Scrap Quilting
MADE EASY

Edited by
Sandra L. Hatch

HOUSE of
WHITE
BIRCHES
PUBLISHERS
SINCE 1947

Scrap Quilting Made Easy

Editor: Sandra L. Hatch

Associate Editor: Jeanne Stauffer

Technical Artist: Connie Rand

Copy Editor: Cathy Reef

Photography: Scott Campbell, Tammy Coquat-Payne, Nora Elsesser

Production Manager: Vicki Macy

Creative Coordinator: Shaun Venish

Production Artist: Brenda Gallmeyer

Production Coordinator: Sandra Beres

Production Assistants: Carol Dailey, Cheryl Lynch

Book Design: Becky Sarasin

Publishers: Carl H. Muselman, Arthur K. Muselman

Chief Executive Officer: John Robinson

Marketing Director: Scott Moss

Editorial Director: Vivian Rothe

Production Director: Scott Smith

Printed in the United States of America

First Printing: 1997

Library of Congress Number: 96-78456

ISBN: 882138-23-6

Every effort has been made to ensure the accuracy and completeness of the instructions in this book. However, we cannot be responsible for human error or for the results when using materials other than those specified in the instructions, or for variations in individual work.

Cover quilt: *Exploding Star*, page 46

Scrap Fun

Scrap quilts from the past were often made from fabrics cut from worn-out clothing. Every piece of available fabric was recycled into quilts. If you examine an old quilt, you will often find that even the smallest patch was pieced together from several smaller pieces of the same fabric to create a patch large enough to fit what was needed.

Today scrap quilts are often made from new fabrics. Sometimes the fabric is purchased as quarter-yard or fat-quarter pieces, and sometimes the scraps are left over from previous sewing or quilting projects. Sure, we still cut up worn-out clothing, but it is not our main source of scraps anymore.

A successful scrap quilt uses hundreds of fabrics. These can be in one color family or a mixture of colors. The design is determined by the placement of lights and darks. The key to success is in the mixing of different color values.

Before you choose a pattern, get your scrap collection in order. The collection process is fun. Sort your scraps by color, size, strips, stitched units, etc. You will soon see what your favorite colors are as that particular scrap pile will be bigger than all the rest.

If you have not been saving scraps for a long time, purchase fat-quarter pieces in your chosen color scheme. Look for these in bundles at regional quilt shows where vendors have done the work for you in putting matching colors together.

Visit secondhand clothing stores; look for cotton shirts and dresses which might yield a good assortment of fabric. Check out yard sales where it is possible you'll find a box of fabric—a real treasure.

If you still need a wider variety of scraps than your collection provides, swap with fellow quilters. Trade fabric in squares or strips, one for one. If you are a member of a group of 20 people and each one shares 20 squares of different fabrics, your collection will grow by 400 squares in one swap. If you are short on Christmas prints, for example, ask your friends to bring twenty 3" squares of Christmas prints to your next meeting. After swapping, you might have enough squares to complete a whole quilt.

Scrap quilts can be made in units or blocks. They can be tied together with a common background fabric or sashing and border strips. They can grow larger as you stitch, and running out of one fabric is nearly impossible, since no one fabric is important.

Whether you choose to make a small wall quilt or a bed-size quilt, if you have never made a scrap quilt before, you are in for a real treat. Set aside all of your preconceived notions about matching fabrics and color coordination and experiment. Enjoy the process—have some fun!

Sandra L. Hatch

Contents

Memories of Grandmother

Glorious Scrap Quilts

A Happy Scrappy Christmas

Special-Occasion Quilts

General Instructions

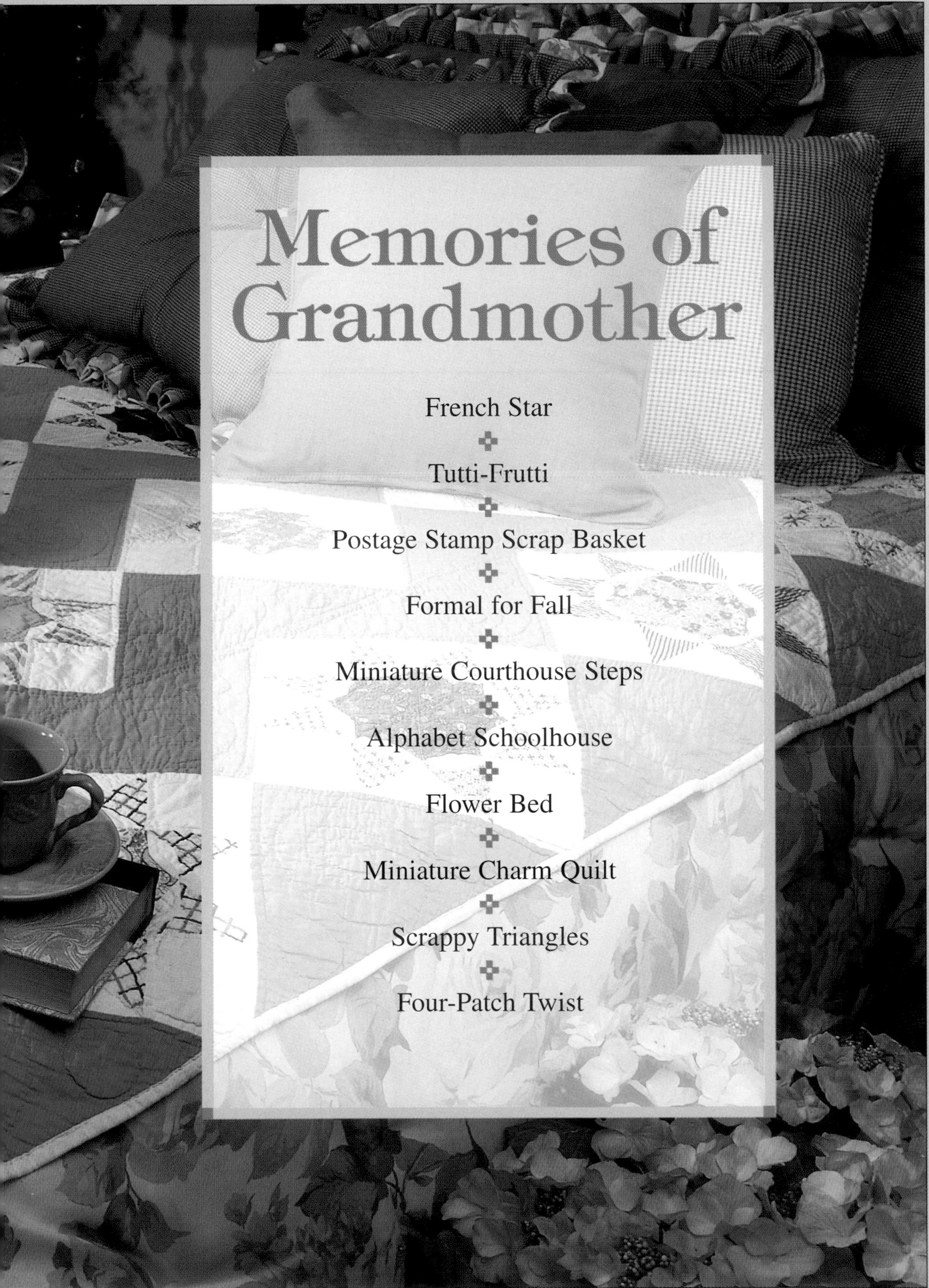

Memories of Grandmother

French Star

✤

Tutti-Frutti

✤

Postage Stamp Scrap Basket

✤

Formal for Fall

✤

Miniature Courthouse Steps

✤

Alphabet Schoolhouse

✤

Flower Bed

✤

Miniature Charm Quilt

✤

Scrappy Triangles

✤

Four-Patch Twist

French Star

*The quilt shown was machine-pieced and hand-quilted in the 1930s.
Its maker is unknown. In the book* One Hundred and One Patchwork Patterns
*by Ruby McKim, information provided with the pattern states that the
French Star is a Canadian variation of the Eight-Pointed Star.*

PROJECT SPECIFICATIONS
Skill Level: Intermediate

Quilt Size: Approximately 70 1/2" x 84 3/4"

Block Size: 10" x 10"

Number of Blocks Needed: 28 whole blocks and
4 half-blocks

MATERIALS

French Star
10" x 10" Block

- 2 1/4 yards total assorted scraps
- 2 3/4 yards white solid for background
- 3 yards blue solid for sashing
- Backing 74" x 89"
- Batting 74" x 89"
- 8 1/2 yards self-made or purchased binding
- Neutral-color all-purpose thread
- 1 spool quilting thread
- Basic sewing and quilting supplies

INSTRUCTIONS
Note: A 1/4" seam allowance is used throughout.

Cutting
Step 1. Prepare templates for pattern pieces given. Cut as directed on each piece to create one block (whole quilt) or half-block (whole quilt). You will need 28 whole and four half-blocks to complete the quilt as shown. *Note: To eliminate the need to cut individual pieces for A and B, fabric strips may be used. For A cut eight strips white 3 7/16" by fabric width. Cut each strip into 3 7/16" segments for A; repeat for 112 A pieces. For B, cut three strips 5 5/16" by fabric width. Cut each strip into 5 5/16" segments. Cut each segment on both diagonals to make four B triangles from each square; repeat for 132 B pieces.*

Step 2. Cut 58 squares blue solid 8" x 8". Cut each square in half once to make G corner triangles as shown in Figure 1.

Figure 1
Cut 8" x 8" squares in half on the diagonal for G.

Piecing Blocks
Step 1. To piece one block, sew D to C; repeat for eight C-D units. Sew two C-D units to each E; repeat for four units.

Step 2. Join the C-D-E units to make star shape. Set in A squares and B triangles to complete the block referring to Figure 2; press. Repeat for 28 blocks.

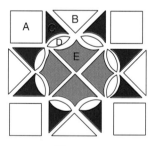

Figure 2
Sew pieces together to make whole blocks.

Step 3. For half-blocks, join two C-D-E units; set in one A and four B pieces as shown in Figure 3; press. Repeat for four half-blocks.

Figure 3
Sew pieces together to make half-blocks.

Quilt Top Assembly

Step 1. Sew a blue solid G triangle to each side of each whole block as shown in Figure 4; press seams toward G. *Note: In the quilt shown, the blue triangles are missing from each corner of the quilt.*

Step 2. Sew a blue solid G triangle to two sides of each half-block as shown in Figure 5.

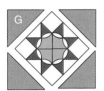

Figure 4
Sew a G triangle to each side of each whole block.

Figure 5
Sew a G triangle to each side of half-blocks.

Step 3. Arrange whole blocks in three rows of six blocks each referring to Figure 6; join the blocks in rows; press.

Step 4. Arrange five whole blocks in a row with a

Figure 6
Arrange blocks in 3 rows of 6 blocks and 2 rows of 5 whole blocks and 2 half-blocks.

half-block at each end as shown in Figure 6. Join the blocks in rows; press. Repeat for two rows.

Step 5. Arrange the whole-block rows with the half-block rows referring to the Placement Diagram and Figure 6; join the rows; press.

Finishing

Step 1. Prepare pieced top for quilting referring to Chapter 5.

Step 2. Mark quilting design given onto G triangles as shown in Figure 7. Quilt in the ditch of the seams of the blocks, 1/4" inside each block shape, on marked lines and as desired by hand or machine.

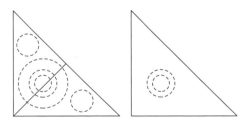

Figure 7
Mark quilting designs on G triangles as shown.

Step 3. When quilting is complete finish edges referring to Chapter 5.

—By Carol Scherer

French Star
Placement Diagram
Approximately 70 1/2" x 84 3/4"

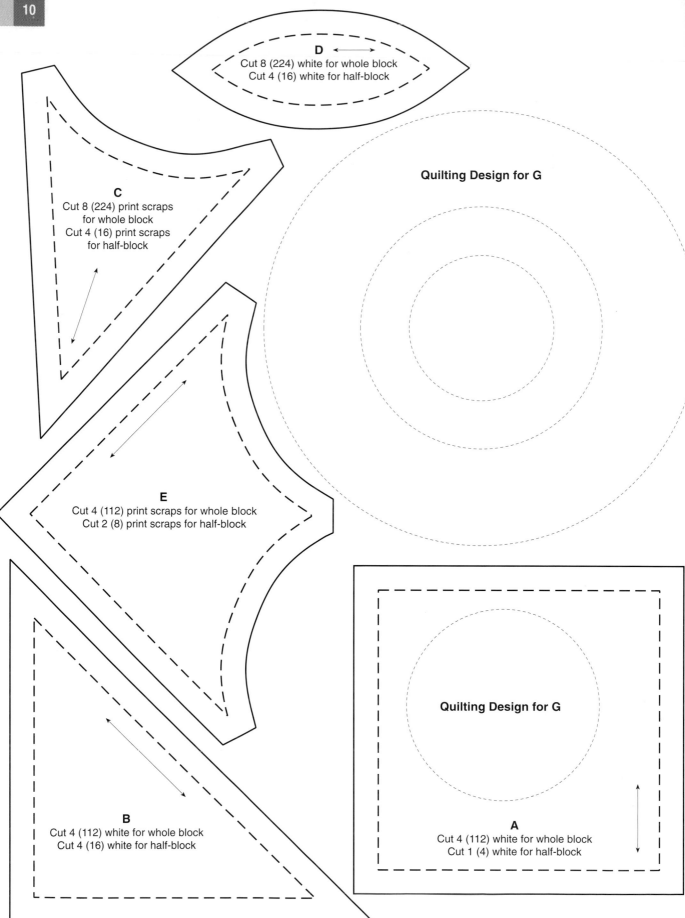

D
Cut 8 (224) white for whole block
Cut 4 (16) white for half-block

Quilting Design for G

C
Cut 8 (224) print scraps
for whole block
Cut 4 (16) print scraps
for half-block

E
Cut 4 (112) print scraps for whole block
Cut 2 (8) print scraps for half-block

Quilting Design for G

B
Cut 4 (112) white for whole block
Cut 4 (16) white for half-block

A
Cut 4 (112) white for whole block
Cut 1 (4) white for half-block

Scrap Quilting Made Easy

Tutti-Frutti

Collect 1"-wide strips of fabrics from your scrap basket to make this scrumptious-looking miniature quilt. The fabrics used in the quilt shown here are from the '30s. The quilt is quick and easy to make by machine.

PROJECT SPECIFICATIONS

Skill Level: Beginner
Quilt Size: Approximately 13 7/8" x 16 3/4"
Block Size: 2 7/8" x 2 7/8"
Number of Blocks Needed: 12

MATERIALS

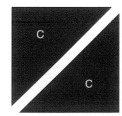

Tutti Frutti
2 7/8" x 2 7/8" Block

- 4" x 4" square each of 24 assorted light, medium and dark fabric scraps
- 4" x 7" piece each of 12 assorted light, medium and dark fabric strips
- 13" x 14" scrap solid for borders
- 8" x 8" square dark solid for border corners
- 6" x 18" piece fabric for binding
- Backing 17" x 20"
- Batting 17" x 20"
- Neutral-color all-purpose thread
- 1 spool quilting thread
- Basic sewing and quilting supplies

INSTRUCTIONS

Note: A 1/4" seam allowance is used throughout.

Cutting

Step 1. Stack the 4" x 4" fabric scraps; cut two strips 1" x 2 1/2" from each square for pieces A and B.

Step 2. Stack the 4" x 7" fabric scraps; cut two squares 2 1/2" x 2 1/2" from each scrap for C.

Step 3. Cut two strips border fabric 2 7/8" x 12" for D and two strips 2 7/8" x 9 1/8" for E.

Step 4. Cut four squares 2 7/8" x 2 7/8" from 8" x 8" dark solid for F border corners.

Step 5. Cut two strips binding fabric 1" x 17" and two strips 1" x 16".

Block Assembly

Note: Press seams in the direction of the arrows as indicated on drawings or as instructed.

Step 1. Sew two matching A strips with two matching B strips as shown in Figure 1; repeat for 12 sets.

Step 2. Stack the assorted C squares; cut in half once on the diagonal to make triangles as shown in Figure 2.

Figure 1
Sew 2 A and 2 B pieces together.

Figure 2
Cut C squares on the diagonal to make triangles.

Step 3. Sew four matching triangles to the sides of an A-B set as shown in Figure 3. Repeat for 12 blocks. Square up blocks to 2 7/8" x 2 7/8", if necessary.

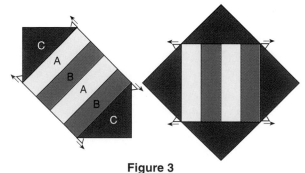

Figure 3
Sew 4 matching triangles to the A-B unit.

Quilt Top Assembly

Step 1. Arrange the blocks in four rows of three blocks each as shown in Figure 4. Join the blocks in rows; press. Join the rows to complete center; press.

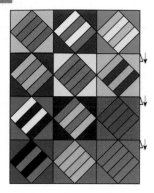

Figure 4
Arrange blocks in rows.

Step 2. Sew the D border strips to the long sides of the pieced center; press.

Step 3. Sew an F square to each end of the E border strips. Sew to top and bottom; press.

Finishing

Step 1. Mark the quilting design given for borders on pieced top using a water-erasable marker or pencil.

Step 2. Prepare pieced top for quilting referring to Chapter 5.

Step 3. Quilt in the ditch of the seams of the blocks, on marked lines and as desired on borders by hand or machine.

Step 4. When quilting is complete, use previously cut binding strips to finish edges referring to Chapter 5.

—*By Chris Carlson*

Border Quilting Design

Tutti-Frutti
Placement Diagram
Approximately 13 7/8" x 16 3/4"
(includes binding)

Postage Stamp Scrap Basket

Many years ago the postal service printed a stamp using this antique scrap quilt block as the basis for the design. This pattern has been popular over the years. The block is small and uses tiny scraps from your real basket of fabric tidbits.

QUILT SPECIFICATIONS
Skill Level: Intermediate
Quilt Size: 21 1/2" x 21 1/2"
Block Size: 4" x 4"

MATERIALS

Postage Stamp
4" x 4" Block

- 1/8 yard each or scraps of 4 coordinated rose prints, 4 coordinated teal prints and 4–6 coordinated beige prints for background
- 1/8 yard dark contrasting fabric for narrow inner borders
- 1/2 yard medium print for outer borders and binding
- Backing 24" x 24"
- Batting 24" x 24"
- All-purpose thread to match fabrics
- 1 spool contrasting quilting thread
- Basic sewing supplies and tools, rotary cutter, mat and ruler

INSTRUCTIONS

Step 1. Prepare templates using pattern pieces given. Cut as directed for one block. Repeat for 16 blocks.

Step 2. To complete one block, appliqué the basket handle to a background C piece. Sew this background C to a print C. Sew a print A to a background B; repeat. Sew the A-B units to C-C. Sew a background C to the remaining corner to finish referring to Figure 1; press. Repeat for 16 blocks.

Step 3. Join four basket blocks to make a larger block as shown in Figure 2; press. Repeat for four larger blocks.

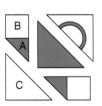

Figure 1
Join pieces to complete 1 block.

Figure 2
Join 4 blocks to make a larger block.

Step 4. Cut two strips dark contrast fabric 1" x 8 1/2". Sew one of these strips between two blocks; repeat. Press seams toward strips.

Step 5. Cut three strips dark contrast fabric 1" x 17". Join the two previously pieced sections with one strip; press seams toward strip. Sew the remaining two strips to the top and bottom of pieced section; press seams toward strips.

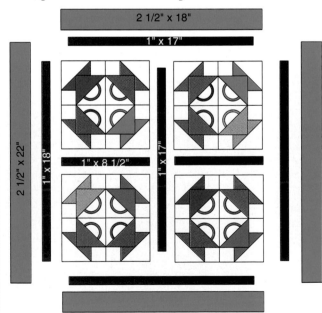

Figure 3
Arrange blocks with strips as shown.

Step 6. Cut two strips dark contrast fabric 1" x 18"; sew a strip to each remaining side. Press seams toward strips.

Step 7. Cut two strips medium fabric 2 1/2" x 18"; sew to top and bottom. Cut two more strips 2 1/2" x 22"; sew to remaining sides. Press seams toward strips. Refer to Figure 3 for strip placement.

Finishing

Step 1. Transfer partial braid quilting pattern to outside border strips, aligning seam with guideline. Also mark 1/4" echo lines within the C pieces and 1/2" echo line within block outer seam lines.

Step 2. Prepare quilt top for quilting referring to Chapter 5.

Step 3. Hand- or machine-quilt on marked lines and in the ditch of all patchwork and appliqué seams as desired using contrasting quilting thread.

Step 4. When quilting is complete, prepare binding and finish edge of quilt referring to Chapter 5 for method choices and instructions.

—By Jodi G. Warner

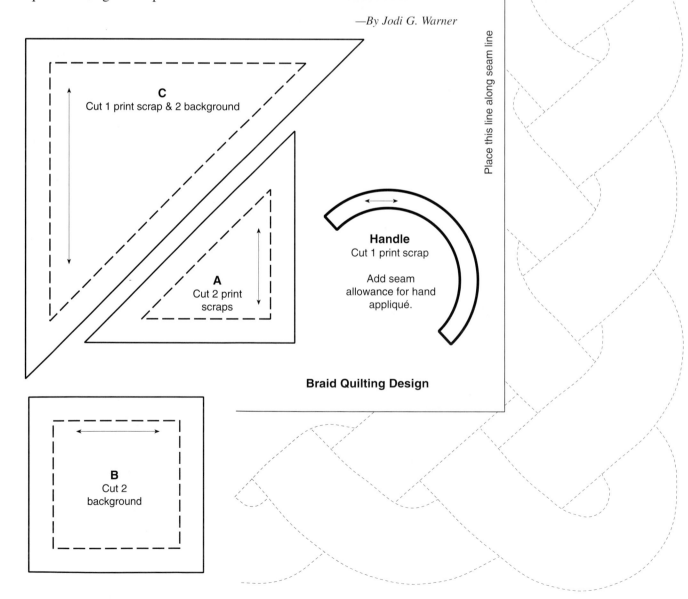

C
Cut 1 print scrap & 2 background

A
Cut 2 print scraps

B
Cut 2 background

Handle
Cut 1 print scrap

Add seam allowance for hand appliqué.

Braid Quilting Design

Place this line along seam line

**Postage Stamp
Scrap Basket**
Placement Diagram
21 1/2" x 21 1/2"
(without binding)

Formal for Fall

Combine earth-tone fabrics to make this bright scrap quilt. Use the same fabric in the center of each Log Cabin block on the border, as a border fabric to separate the pieced center from the border blocks and in the pieced blocks in the center to give it all a coordinated look. The gold, yellow and brown scraps combine to make a beautiful fall wall quilt.

PROJECT SPECIFICATIONS
Skill Level: Easy
Quilt Size: 36" x 36"
Block Size: 4" x 4"

MATERIALS
- 1/4 yard dark brown print
- 1 yard brown print
- 1 yard total assorted gold, yellow and brown scraps
- Backing 40" x 40"
- Batting 40" x 40"
- 1 spool all-purpose thread to match backing
- 1 spool neutral color thread for sewing pieces
- 1 spool gold metallic thread
- Paper to make paper-piecing patterns
- 4 1/4 yards self-made or purchased binding
- Basic sewing and quilting supplies

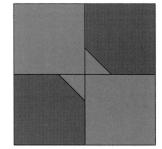

Bow Tie
4" x 4"
Make 36

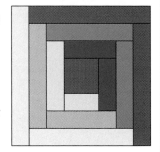

Log Cabin
4" x 4"
Make 32

INSTRUCTIONS
Note: A 1/4" seam allowance is used throughout.

Bow Tie Blocks

Traditional Method
Step 1. Prepare templates for pieces A, B and C. For each block cut two brown print C pieces and two each matching scraps for A and B.

Step 2. Sew a B triangle to each C. Join the B-C units with A to make one block as shown in Figure 1. Repeat for 36 blocks.

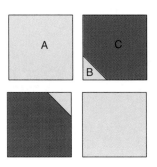

Figure 1
Join units to make 1 block.

Quick Method
Step 1. Cut two squares 2 1/2" x 2 1/2" each from brown print and scraps. Cut two squares 1 5/8" x 1 5/8" from matching scrap.

Step 2. Lay a small square on one corner of a large brown print square. Sew on the diagonal as shown in Figure 2. Trim excess from corner; fold back triangle; press. Repeat with second triangle and a brown print square.

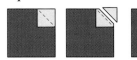

Figure 2
Sew on the diagonal of the small square; trim excess. Fold back to reveal B-C unit.

Step 3. Arrange the pieced units to make one block as shown in Figure 1; repeat for 36 blocks.

Log Cabin Blocks
Step 1. Make 32 copies of full-size paper-piecing pattern given in Figure 3. *Note: The pattern is reversed because stitching is done on the unlined side of the paper which will be the top of the finished block.*

Step 2. Cut fabric scraps in 1"-wide strips of varying lengths.

Miniature Courthouse Steps

Leftover fabric strips can become treasures if you are searching for fabrics to use in this Miniature Courthouse Steps *quilt. Instead of completing the quilt with blocks, this quilt builds around itself to create one Courthouse Steps block in miniature.*

The more variety in colors and prints you use in this *Miniature Courthouse Steps*, the prettier the finished quilt will be.

Using the sew-and-flip paper-piecing method assures accuracy while saving time, but you can use precut strips and still have good results.

Cutting fabric strips on the lengthwise grain of the fabric makes stronger strips. If you are not sure which way the lengthwise grain is on the fabric scrap, grab two opposite sides of the piece and pull.

If it stretches at all, it is not the lengthwise grain; the lengthwise grain threads will not stretch when pulled.

The quilt starts in the center with a square and works out on opposite sides instead of adjacent sides to create the Courthouse Steps variation.

PROJECT SPECIFICATIONS
Skill Level: Easy
Quilt Size: 13" x 13"

MATERIALS
Note: If using paper-piecing methods, fabrics need not be cut to any size in advance as long as they are at least 1" wide and long enough to cover the space. They are trimmed after stitching to fit. Use sizes below as guides for lengths needed, but it is not necessary to accurately cut pieces to these lengths. Refer to the Placement Diagram and photo of sample project for placement of lights and darks. If using precut logs, materials are needed as follows:

- 1 square 1 1/2" x 1 1/2" red print for center
- 2 strips each 1" x 1 1/2" for logs 1 and 2
- 4 strips each 1" x 2 1/2" for logs 3 –6
- 4 strips each 1" x 3 1/2" for logs 7–10
- 4 strips each 1" x 4 1/2" for logs 11–14
- 4 strips each 1" x 5 1/2" for logs 15–18
- 4 strips each 1" x 6 1/2" for logs 19–22
- 4 strips each 1" x 7 1/2" for logs 23–26
- 4 strips each 1" x 8 1/2" for logs 27–30
- 4 strips each 1" x 9 1/2" for logs 31–34
- 4 strips each 1" x 10 1/2" for logs 35–38
- 4 strips each 1" x 11 1/2" for logs 39–42
- 4 strips each 1" x 12 1/2" for logs 43–46
- 2 strips 1" x 13 1/2" for logs 47 and 48
- Backing 13" x 13"
- Batting 13" x 13"
- All-purpose thread to match fabrics
- 6" x 17" fabric piece for binding

Using Precut Logs
Note: Press all seams flat and away from the center square. Square the corners after sewing every four logs to keep project square.

Step 1. Sew matching logs 1 and 2 to left and right sides of the center square as shown in Figure 1.

Figure 1
Sew logs 1 and 2 to opposite sides of the center square.

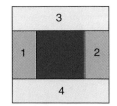

Figure 2
Sew logs 3 and 4 to opposite sides of center square.

Step 2. Sew matching logs 3 and 4 to the upper and lower edges of the pieced section as shown in Figure 2.

Step 3. Continue adding logs 5–48, squaring up the corners after every fourth row.

Step 4. Gently press the top on both sides and trim the edges if necessary.

Step 3. Cut 32 squares brown print 1 1/2" x 1 1/2".

Step 4. Pin a brown print square on the center of the unlined side of one paper-piecing pattern. Pin a light-colored scrap strip in the No. 2 position, lining up edges with the center square. Turn to the lined side of the paper; stitch on the line, beginning a few stitches off the line and stitching past the line at the end as shown in Figure 4. Set stitch length at 14–16 stitches per inch to make small stitches. *Note: Small stitches make it easier to pull the paper away later.*

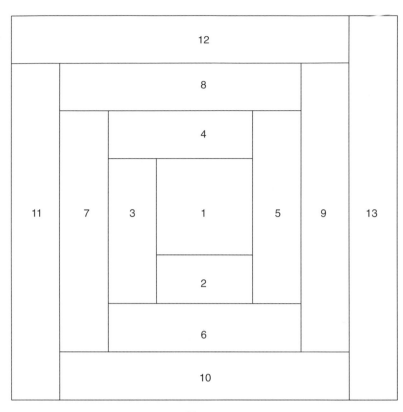

Figure 3
Full-size paper-piecing pattern for Log Cabin blocks.

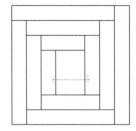

Figure 4
Stitch along line, beginning and ending a few stitches beyond the line. (Drawing shows marked side of paper; patches are stitched on opposite side.)

Step 5. Turn paper to fabric side; flip piece No. 2 up; finger-press flat. Add piece No. 3 using the same method. Continue adding strips in numerical order to finish one unit referring to the photo of the finished project for color suggestions; press. Repeat for 32 blocks; leave paper on blocks.

Assembly

Step 1. Arrange the Bow Tie blocks in six rows of six blocks each referring to Figure 5. Join in rows; join rows to complete pieced center; press.

Step 2. Cut two strips dark brown print 1" x 24 1/2"; sew to top and bottom; press seams toward strips. Cut two more strips 1" x 25 1/2"; sew to the opposite sides; press seams toward strips.

Step 3. Cut two strips brown print 1 1/2" x 25 1/2"; sew to top and bottom; press. Cut two more strips 1 1/2" x 27 1/2"; sew to opposite sides; press.

Step 4. Cut two strips dark brown print 1" x 27 1/2"; sew to top and bottom; press. Cut two more strips 1" x 28 1/2"; sew to sides; press.

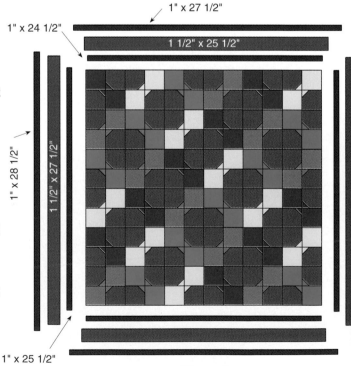

Figure 5
Arrange blocks with strips as shown.

Step 5. Arrange the Log Cabin blocks around pieced center with seven blocks on sides and nine blocks on top and bottom. Join the blocks for sides; press and sew to quilt sides. Join the blocks for top and bottom; press and sew to top and bottom.

Step 6. Press quilt top; trim threads. Remove paper from Log Cabin blocks.

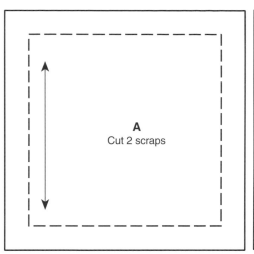

A
Cut 2 scraps

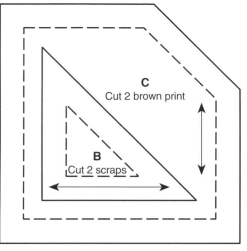

C
Cut 2 brown print

B
Cut 2 scraps

Finishing

Step 1. Prepare pieced section for quilting referring to Chapter 5.

Step 2. Machine-quilt in the ditch of seams using metallic thread in the top of the machine and all-purpose thread to match backing in the bobbin.

Step 3. Prepare quilt for binding and finish edges referring to Chapter 5.

—By Ruth Swasey

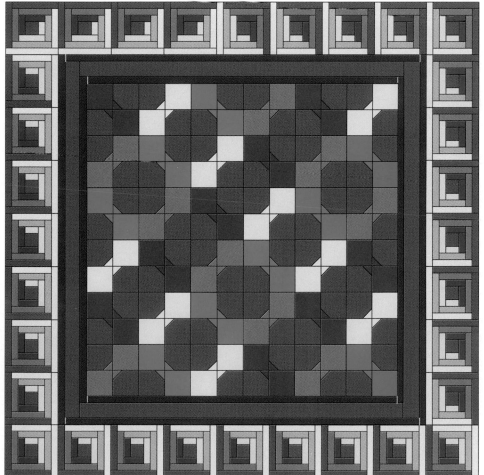

Formal for Fall
Placement Diagram
36" x 36"

Miniature Courthouse Steps

Leftover fabric strips can become treasures if you are searching for fabrics to use in this Miniature Courthouse Steps *quilt. Instead of completing the quilt with blocks, this quilt builds around itself to create one Courthouse Steps block in miniature.*

The more variety in colors and prints you use in this *Miniature Courthouse Steps*, the prettier the finished quilt will be.

Using the sew-and-flip paper-piecing method assures accuracy while saving time, but you can use precut strips and still have good results.

Cutting fabric strips on the lengthwise grain of the fabric makes stronger strips. If you are not sure which way the lengthwise grain is on the fabric scrap, grab two opposite sides of the piece and pull.

If it stretches at all, it is not the lengthwise grain; the lengthwise grain threads will not stretch when pulled.

The quilt starts in the center with a square and works out on opposite sides instead of adjacent sides to create the Courthouse Steps variation.

PROJECT SPECIFICATIONS
Skill Level: Easy
Quilt Size: 13" x 13"

MATERIALS
Note: If using paper-piecing methods, fabrics need not be cut to any size in advance as long as they are at least 1" wide and long enough to cover the space. They are trimmed after stitching to fit. Use sizes below as guides for lengths needed, but it is not necessary to accurately cut pieces to these lengths. Refer to the Placement Diagram and photo of sample project for placement of lights and darks. If using precut logs, materials are needed as follows:

- 1 square 1 1/2" x 1 1/2" red print for center
- 2 strips each 1" x 1 1/2" for logs 1 and 2
- 4 strips each 1" x 2 1/2" for logs 3 –6
- 4 strips each 1" x 3 1/2" for logs 7–10
- 4 strips each 1" x 4 1/2" for logs 11–14
- 4 strips each 1" x 5 1/2" for logs 15–18
- 4 strips each 1" x 6 1/2" for logs 19–22

- 4 strips each 1" x 7 1/2" for logs 23–26
- 4 strips each 1" x 8 1/2" for logs 27–30
- 4 strips each 1" x 9 1/2" for logs 31–34
- 4 strips each 1" x 10 1/2" for logs 35–38
- 4 strips each 1" x 11 1/2" for logs 39–42
- 4 strips each 1" x 12 1/2" for logs 43–46
- 2 strips 1" x 13 1/2" for logs 47 and 48
- Backing 13" x 13"
- Batting 13" x 13"
- All-purpose thread to match fabrics
- 6" x 17" fabric piece for binding

Using Precut Logs
Note: Press all seams flat and away from the center square. Square the corners after sewing every four logs to keep project square.

Step 1. Sew matching logs 1 and 2 to left and right sides of the center square as shown in Figure 1.

Figure 1
Sew logs 1 and 2 to opposite sides of the center square.

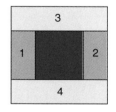

Figure 2
Sew logs 3 and 4 to opposite sides of center square.

Step 2. Sew matching logs 3 and 4 to the upper and lower edges of the pieced section as shown in Figure 2.

Step 3. Continue adding logs 5–48, squaring up the corners after every fourth row.

Step 4. Gently press the top on both sides and trim the edges if necessary.

Step 5. Mark the top for quilting, if necessary. The quilt shown was quilted in the center of every other strip and diagonal from corner to corner.

Step 6. Sandwich batting between completed top and prepared backing piece. Safety-pin or baste layers together to hold flat.

Step 7. Quilt on marked lines and as desired. When quilting is complete, trim edges even and remove basting or pins.

Step 8. Cut the 6" x 17" binding fabric into two 1" x 13 1/2" and two 1" x 15 1/2" strips. Sew a shorter strip to opposite sides of the quilt center, extending the strip an equal amount on both ends. Trim excess even with quilt top, referring to Figure 3. Fold over raw edge 1/4" and turn to backside; hand-stitch in place.

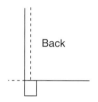

Figure 3
Sew binding strips to
opposite sides of quilt
center; trim ends even.

Step 9. Sew longer strips to the remaining two sides as in Step 8. Trim ends to extend 3/8" beyond end of quilt edge. Fold ends under as shown in Figure 4. Turn to back and hand-stitch in place to finish.

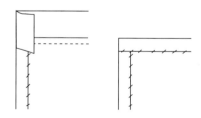

Figure 4
Fold ends under, turn to
back and hand-stitch in
place as shown.

Using Paper-Piecing

Step 1. Use a 15" x 15" piece of 1/4" gridded graph paper or use four 8 1/2" x 11" sheets that are accurately marked and glued together on the backside.

Step 2. Fold the paper in half twice to find the center. Draw a 1" x 1" square in the center. Draw 1/2"-

wide logs, starting with the side logs, then the upper and lower logs as shown in Figure 5. Continue adding lines until you have 12 logs on each side.

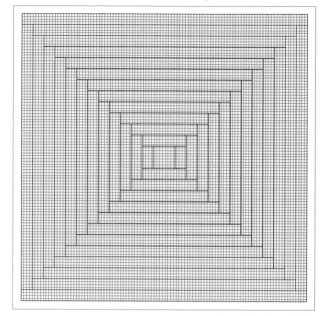

Figure 5
Draw lines 1/2" apart on graph paper to
make 12 rounds as shown.

Step 3. Number the logs from 1–48. *Note: All logs are sewn with right sides facing the backside of the pattern.* Pin the seams of longer logs flat as you sew for a smoother appearance.

Step 4. Refer to Chapter 5 for paper-piecing instructions. Center and tack the 1 1/2" center square to the backside of the paper pattern with a basting stitch, wrong sides together, as shown in Figure 6.

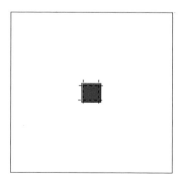

Figure 6
Place square on backside of paper; baste in place.

Step 5. Sew matching 1 and 2 logs to the left and right edges of the square as shown in Figure 7.

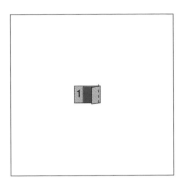

Figure 7
Sew logs 1 and 2 in place.

Step 6. Continue adding logs in numerical order, trimming each log seam to 1/4" after sewing, until 12 logs have been added to each side. Press each log flat before adding next log.

Step 7. Gently remove the paper foundation from the backside of the quilt top, using the tip of a seam ripper to start the ripping process.

Step 8. Finish as instructed in Steps 5–9 for precut method.

—By Chris Carlson

Miniature Courthouse Steps
Placement Diagram
13" x 13"

Alphabet Schoolhouse

"School days, school days, good old Golden Rule days." Make each schoolhouse from different fabrics and use scraps in the border pieces to create a balanced but scrappy wall quilt for a teacher or student or anyone with fond memories of the days of readin', writin' and 'rithmetic.

QUILT SPECIFICATIONS
Skill Level: Intermediate
Quilt Size: 29 1/2" x 29 1/2"
Block Size: 8" x 8"
Number of Blocks: 4

MATERIALS
- 1 yard background fabric
- 1/8 yard each 16 coordinated prints for house pieces and border diamonds
- 3/8 yard cream ticking stripe for binding
- All-purpose thread to match fabrics
- Backing 33" x 33"
- Batting 33" x 33"

Alphabet Schoolhouse
8" x 8" Block

INSTRUCTIONS
Step 1. Prepare templates using pattern pieces given. Cut as directed on each piece for one block; repeat for four blocks. *Note: Trace templates onto the wrong side of the fabric. Pieces K, J and N must be turned over when traced.*

Step 2. To piece one block, sew A to B to A to B to A. Add C, D, E and F referring to Figure 1.

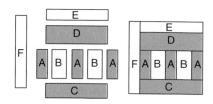

Figure 1
Sew A, B, C, D, E and F
pieces together as shown.

Step 3. Sew K to J and M to L to M. Join these two units as shown in Figure 2.

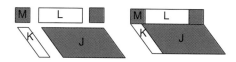

Figure 2
Sew K, J, L and M pieces
together as shown.

Step 4. Sew G to H to G; add I as shown in Figure 3.

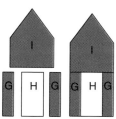

Figure 3
Sew G, H and I pieces
together as shown.

Step 5. Arrange units and join, adding N and NR as shown in Figure 4 to complete one block; repeat for four blocks. Press and square up to 8 1/2" x 8 1/2", if necessary.

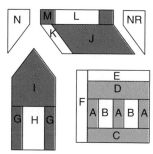

Figure 4
Join the pieced units and set on
N and NR to complete 1 block.

Assembly
Step 1. Cut six strips background 2" x 8 1/2" for O. Arrange two blocks with three O strips to make a row referring to Figure 5. Join the pieces to make one row; repeat for second row.

Step 2. Cut three strips background 2" x 21" for P. Sew a strip between two block rows; sew the remaining strips to the sides of the pieced section as shown in Figure 5.

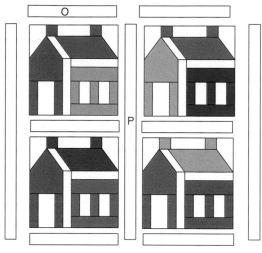

Figure 5
Join blocks with O strips. Join rows with P strips.

Step 3. Cut border pieces Q, R and S as directed on each piece. Join Q with R and QR to make a row using seven R pieces as shown in Figure 6; repeat for four border strips.

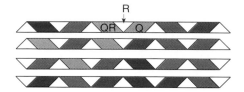

Figure 6
Sew Q and R together to make a strip as shown; repeat for 4 strips.

Step 4. Sew a strip to each side of the pieced center. Sew S to each corner; press.

Step 5. Cut four strips background fabric 4" x 30" for borders. Sew a strip to each side, mitering corners. Use pattern given to create rounded corners; press.

Finishing

Step 1. Prepare quilt top for quilting referring to instructions on Chapter 5.

Step 2. Mark the heart shape on the I pieces in each block, the alphabet and "HOME SWEET HOME" and interlocking hearts quilting patterns onto the outside border strips, positioning dashed base lines 3/4" away from pieced border seam. Mark cross-hatch quilting lines through the background of the blocks including doors and windows using a 3/4" grid.

Step 3. Quilt on marked lines by hand or machine.

Step 4. Prepare binding from cream ticking stripe referring to Chapter 5. Finish edges referring to Chapter 5, easing binding as necessary on corners.

—By Jodi Warner

Alphabet Schoolhouse
Placement Diagram
29 1/2" x 29 1/2"

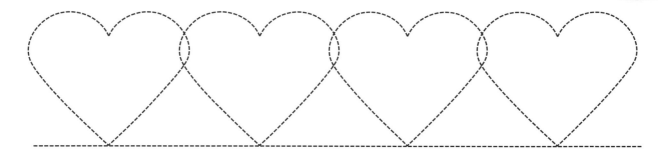

Heart Quilting Pattern
Place on borders, overlapping as shown.

ABCD

EFGH

IJKL

Alphabet Letters
Use for quilting design; position dashed line 3/4" above seam line on borders

M N O P

Q R S T

U V W

X Y Z

A
Cut 3

S
Cut 4 scraps

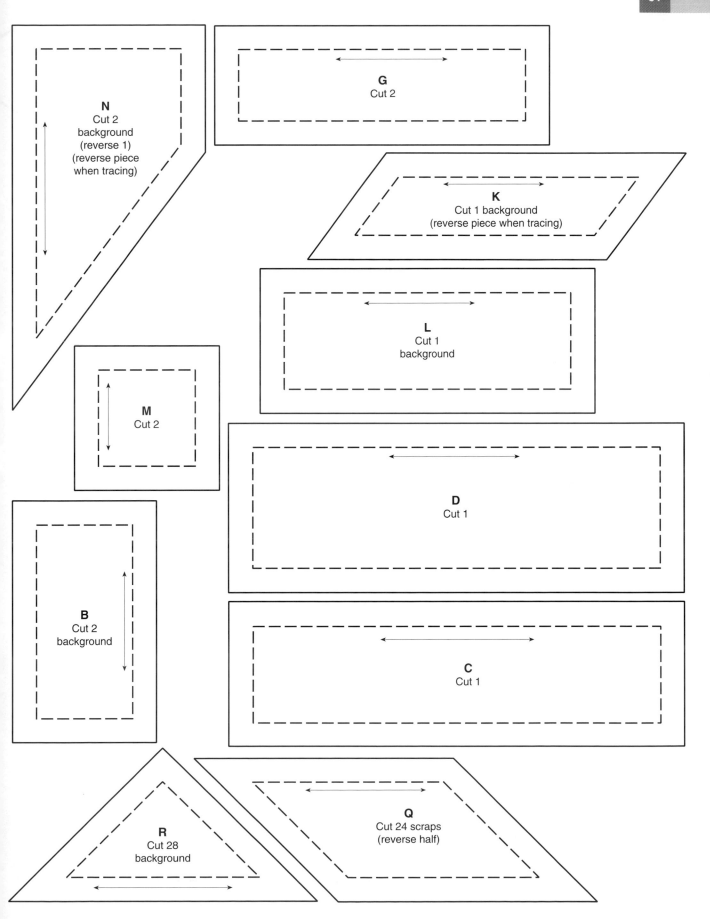

N
Cut 2
background
(reverse 1)
(reverse piece
when tracing)

G
Cut 2

K
Cut 1 background
(reverse piece when tracing)

L
Cut 1
background

M
Cut 2

D
Cut 1

B
Cut 2
background

C
Cut 1

R
Cut 28
background

Q
Cut 24 scraps
(reverse half)

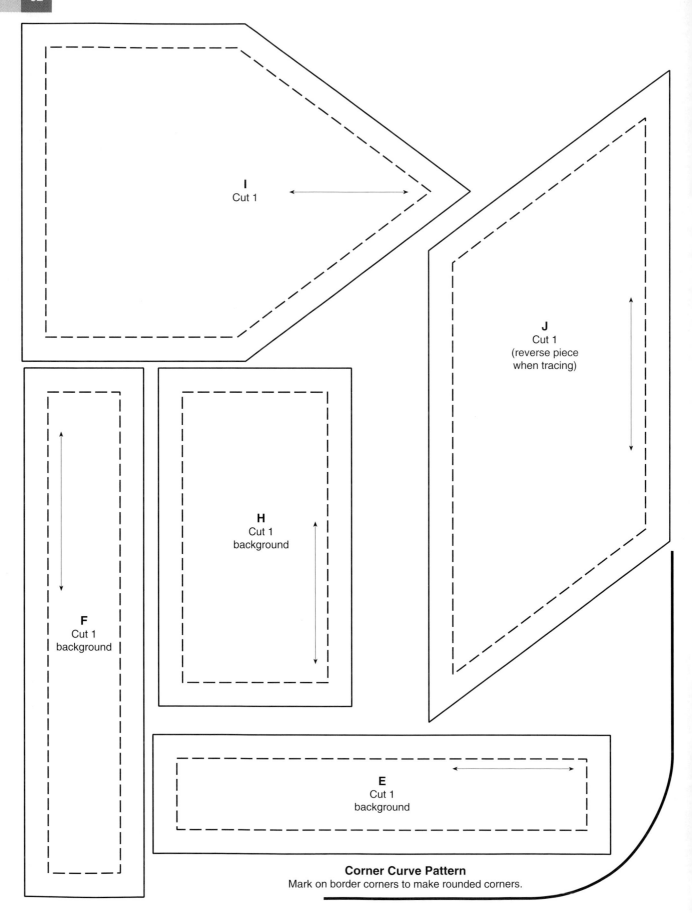

I
Cut 1

J
Cut 1
(reverse piece
when tracing)

F
Cut 1
background

H
Cut 1
background

E
Cut 1
background

Corner Curve Pattern
Mark on border corners to make rounded corners.

Flower Bed

Pick an array of colorful floral prints and sew this quick project for a cheery miniature quilt. Quick-cut triangles are used to make the flowers. Use the leftovers to make an identical quilt to use as a gift. Vintage fabrics were chosen to give this tiny quilt an old-fashioned look.

PROJECT SPECIFICATIONS
Skill Level: Intermediate
Quilt Size: 10" x 11 1/2"
Block Size: 1 1/2" x 1 1/2"
Number of Blocks Needed: 20

MATERIALS
- 5" x 5" piece each of 20 assorted prints
- 6" x 10" piece pink solid for sashing
- 9" x 12" piece green-and-pink print for borders
- 6" x 13" piece purple-and-white print for binding
- 16" x 18" piece muslin
- Backing 14" x 16"
- Lightweight batting 14" x 15"
- Neutral color all-purpose thread
- Basic sewing and quilting supplies, 6" square ruler and 3" x 18" ruler

Flower Bed
Placement Diagram
1 1/2" x 1 1/2" Block
(Actual Size)

INSTRUCTIONS
Note: A 1/4" seam allowance is used throughout. Cut all strips on the lengthwise grain if possible.

Cutting
Step 1. Stack the 20 assorted print squares; cut from each piece: one square 1 3/8" x 1 3/8" for A and one square 2 3/8" x 2 3/8" for B.

Step 2. Cut five strips muslin 1" x 12" for C and five strips 1" x 16" for D.

Step 3. Cut two strips 1" x 8" for E and two strips 1" x 7 1/2" for F from pink solid.

Step 4. Cut two strips 1 3/4" x 9" for G and two strips 1 3/4" x 10" for H from green-and-pink print.

Step 5. Cut two strips 1" x 11 1/2" and two strips

1" x 12" from purple-and-white print for binding.

Block Assembly
Note: Press seams in the direction of the arrows as indicated on drawings or as instructed.

Step 1. Stack the 20 assorted A squares. Cut in half once on the diagonal to make 40 triangles. Set aside one triangle from each print.

Step 2. Sew four of the assorted triangles to one muslin C strip starting about 1" down from the top edge and leaving about 1" space between each triangle to make one set referring to Figure 1. Make a total of five sets. Press triangles away from strip with seam toward triangles.

Step 3. Using the ruler, continue the angle of the triangle on the strip as shown in Figure 2. Cut to make 20 pieced triangle sets; trim seams to 1/8".

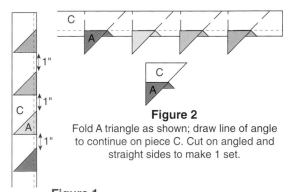

Figure 2
Fold A triangle as shown; draw line of angle to continue on piece C. Cut on angled and straight sides to make 1 set.

Figure 1
Sew A triangles to muslin C strips, leaving about 1" between pieces.

Step 4. Sew four of these assorted sets to one muslin D strip, starting about 1/2" down from the top edges and leaving about 1" between each set to make one set as shown in Figure 3. Press the seams toward triangles.

Step 5. Using a ruler, continue the angle of the triangle on the strip as shown in Figure 4. Cut to make 20 pieced triangle sets; trim seams to 1/8".

Step 6. Stack the 20 assorted B triangles; cut in half once on the diagonal for a total of 40 triangles. Set aside one triangle from each print.

Step 7. Sew a matching triangle cut in Step 6 to a matching triangle set made in Step 5 to complete one Flower Bed block as shown in Figure 5. Repeat to complete 20 blocks; press seams open on both sides and trim rabbit ears. Square up blocks to 2", if necessary.

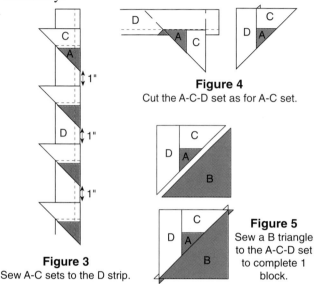

Figure 3
Sew A-C sets to the D strip.

Figure 4
Cut the A-C-D set as for A-C set.

Figure 5
Sew a B triangle to the A-C-D set to complete 1 block.

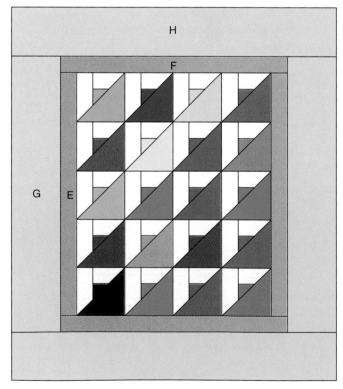

Flower Bed
Placement Diagram
10" x 11 1/2"
(includes binding)

Quilt Top Assembly

Step 1. Arrange the blocks in five horizontal rows of four blocks each. Join the blocks to make rows as shown in Figure 6; press seams open. Join the rows, matching block seams; press all seams in the same direction.

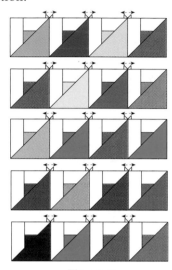

Figure 6
Join blocks to make rows.

Step 2. Sew an E strip (1" x 8") to the left and right sides of the pieced top; press seams toward strips. Repeat with the F strips (1" x 7 1/2") on the top and bottom.

Step 3. Sew a G strip (1 3/4" x 9") to the left and right sides of the pieced top; press seams toward border strips. Repeat with the H strips (1 3/4" x 10") to the top and bottom.

Step 4. Steam-press the quilt top on both sides; check for proper seam pressing and trim loose threads.

Finishing

Step 1. Prepare pieced top for quilting referring to Chapter 5.

Step 2. Quilt in the ditch of the seams of the blocks and as desired by hand or machine.

Step 3. When quilting is complete, use previously cut binding strips to finish edges referring to Chapter 5.

—By Chris Carlson

Miniature Charm Quilt

A charm quilt is the ultimate scrap quilt, for no fabric is repeated. Collecting scraps for a miniature charm quilt is easier than for a full-size one. This one uses only 95 different scraps. If making a larger version you would need thousands of different fabrics to create a true charm quilt. The process of collecting these fabrics is almost as much fun as putting them together into a quilt!

PROJECT SPECIFICATIONS
Skill Level: Intermediate
Quilt Size: 17" x 21"
Unit Size: 1 1/2" x 1 3/4"

MATERIALS
- 15 1/2" x 19 1/2" piece light green solid
- Scraps of 95 different floral prints
- Green print backing 19" x 23"
- Batting 19" x 23"
- Neutral color all-purpose thread
- 1 spool matching quilting thread

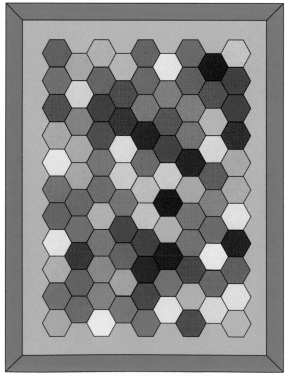

Miniature Charm Quilt
Placement Diagram
17" x 21"

- Freezer paper and see-through template plastic
- Basic sewing and quilting supplies

INSTRUCTIONS
Note: A 1/4" seam allowance is used throughout.

Cutting
Step 1. Trace pattern onto see-through template plastic; cut out. Isolate a flower or design motif on each scrap; place template on wrong side of fabric; trace. Add a 1/4" seam allowance on all sides; cut out.

Step 2. Cut 95 paper templates from freezer paper. For each hexagon, place freezer-paper shape, shiny side up, on wrong side of fabric shape. Turn and press seam allowances down to freezer paper as shown in Figure 1. Repeat for all 95 shapes.

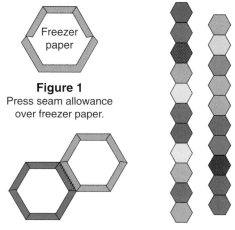

Figure 1
Press seam allowance
over freezer paper.

Figure 3
Whipstitch units together
as shown.

Figure 2
Arrange units in rows.

Piecing the Units
Step 1. Lay out hexagon shapes in five rows of 11 hexagons each and four rows of 10 hexagons each referring to Figure 2.

Step 2. Hand-piece hexagon units together, whip-stitching one piece to another as shown in Figure 3. Join units in rows; join rows to complete the pieced section referring to the Placement Diagram.

Assembly

Step 1. Center pieced section on the 15 1/2" x 19 1/2" piece of light green solid; pin and baste in place.

Step 2. Appliqué the pieced section to the light green solid background.

Step 3. When appliqué is complete, carefully trim away the light green layer underneath the pieced, appliquéd section to reduce bulk.

Step 4. Remove freezer paper from behind each hexagon.

Hexagon
Cut 95 fabric &
95 freezer
paper

Finishing

Step 1. Center batting on wrong side of backing piece; center top section on batting piece. Baste layers in place to hold flat.

Step 2. Quilt 1/4" inside each hexagon and around the outside of the appliquéd section. Add more quilting as desired.

Step 3. When quilting is complete, trim batting 1 3/4" larger all around than quilt top. Trim backing to extend 1 1/4" beyond batting (2 1/2" larger than quilt top).

Step 4. Turn edge of backing under 1/4"; press. Turn backing to the front edge of quilt top; pin in place.

Step 5. Blind-stitch backing to quilt front, mitering corners, to finish.

—By Janice McKee

Scrappy Triangles

This quilt was hand-pieced in the 1930s. The solid red blocks combine with scrap blocks to create a wonderful quilt. The fun part is that the block uses only one size triangle. Collect scraps from all your friends and make a quilt to remind you of them.

PROJECT SPECIFICATIONS

Skill Level: Beginner
Quilt Size: 77 1/2" x 84"
Block Size: 6 1/2" x 6 1/2"
Number of Blocks Needed: 132

MATERIALS

- 4 1/2 yards total assorted light print scraps
- 2 3/4 yards total assorted medium-to-dark print scraps
- 4 3/4 yards red solid
- Backing 81" x 88"
- Batting 81" x 88"
- 9 1/2 yards self-made or purchased binding
- Neutral-color all-purpose thread
- 1 spool quilting thread
- Basic sewing and quilting supplies

INSTRUCTIONS

Note: A 1/4" seam allowance is used throughout.

Scrappy Triangles Block 1
6 1/2" x 6 1/2" Block

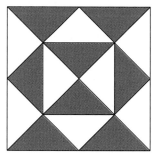

Scrappy Triangles Block 2
6 1/2" x 6 1/2" Block

Cutting

Step 1. Cut seven strips red solid 4 1/2" by fabric width. Cut each strip into ten 4 1/2" segments.

Step 2. Cut 132 squares 4 1/2" x 4 1/2" from light print and 66 squares dark print.

Step 3. Cut 11 strips red solid 3 1/8" by fabric width. Cut each strip into thirteen 3 1/8" segments.

Step 4. Cut 264 squares light print and 132 squares dark print 3 1/8" x 3 1/8".

Step 5. Cut two strips red 3 1/2" x 72" and two strips 3 1/2" x 84 1/2" for borders; set aside.

Piecing Blocks

Step 1. To piece Block 1, place a red 4 1/2" x 4 1/2" square on a same-size light square with right sides together.

Step 2. Draw a line through both diagonals. Sew 1/4" on each side of one diagonal line as shown in Figure 1.

Step 3. Cut squares apart on each diagonal to reveal four sewn A-A triangles with straight of grain on the longest side as shown in Figure 2.

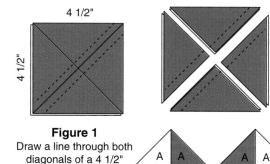

Figure 1
Draw a line through both diagonals of a 4 1/2" square. Sew 1/4" on each side of 1 line.

Figure 2
Cut square apart on both diagonals to reveal 4 A-A triangles (note there are 2 of each color version).

Step 4. Place a red 3 1/8" square on a same-size light square with right sides together.

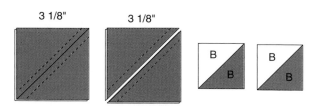

Figure 3
Draw a line through 1 diagonal of a 3 1/8" square. Sew 1/4" on each side of the line. Cut on the drawn line to reveal 2 B-B triangle/squares.

Step 5. Draw one diagonal line. Sew 1/4" on each side of the line. Cut apart on the drawn line to reveal two B-B triangle/squares with straight of grain on the short sides as shown in Figure 3.

Step 6. Arrange the A-A triangles with the B-B triangles as shown in Figure 4. Sew B-B units to make a square; sew A-A units on each side to complete Block 1. Repeat for 66 Block 1 squares.

Figure 4
Arrange the pieced units as shown.

Step 7. Repeat Steps 1–6 using light and dark print scraps to complete Block 2. Repeat for 66 Block 2 squares.

Quilt Top Assembly

Step 1. Arrange the pieced blocks in 12 rows of 11 blocks each, alternating Block 1 and Block 2, referring to the Placement Diagram for arrangement of blocks.

Step 2. Join blocks in rows; press. Join rows; press.

Step 3. Sew the short red border strips to the top and bottom of the pieced center; press seams toward border strips. Sew the longer strips to remaining sides; press seams toward strips.

Finishing

Step 1. Prepare pieced top for quilting referring to Chapter 5.

Step 2. Quilt or tie layers together as desired.

Step 3. When quilting or tying is complete, finish edges referring to Chapter 5.

—By Sandra L. Hatch

Scrappy Triangles
Placement Diagram
77 1/2" x 84"

Four-Patch Twist

When I purchased this quilt as a top it was very stiff, and the fabrics felt starched, so I decided to wash it. Several pieces of red ran, and the color migrated into adjoining pieces. Fortunately I had some fabrics from the same time period and I was able to replace the damaged patches. My mother, my husband and I placed the top on a frame and together we tied it in one day. It was a memorable experience for all of us!

PROJECT SPECIFICATIONS
Skill Level: Beginner
Quilt Size: 66" x 74"
Block Size: 4" x 4"
Number of Blocks Needed: 144 Block 1 and
  144 Block 2

MATERIALS
- 7 yards total of assorted light and dark print scraps
- Backing 70" x 78"
- Batting 70" x 78"
- Neutral-color all-purpose thread
- 3 skeins each white and navy embroidery floss
- Basic sewing and quilting supplies

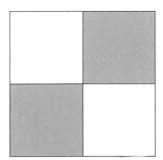

Four-Patch Twist Block 1
4" x 4" Block

INSTRUCTIONS
Note: A 1/4" seam allowance is used throughout.

Piecing Blocks
Step 1. Cut two squares 2 1/2" x 2 1/2" each from a light print and a medium or dark print. Sew

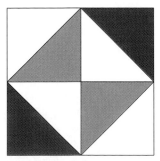

Four-Patch Twist Block 2
4" x 4" Block

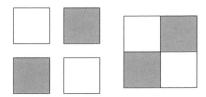

Figure 1
Sew 2 1/2" squares
together to make Block 1.

together to make Block 1 as shown in Figure 1. Repeat for 144 blocks.

Step 2. Cut one square each 2 7/8" x 2 7/8" from two light prints and two dark prints. Place one light and one dark square with right sides together. Draw a line on the diagonal.

Step 3. Sew 1/4" on each side of the diagonal line as shown in Figure 2. Cut apart on drawn line to reveal two triangle/squares as shown in Figure 2; repeat for each light and dark combination.

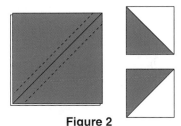

Figure 2
Sew 1/4" on each side of the drawn line.

Step 4. Arrange the triangle/squares as shown in Figure 3 for Block 2. Repeat for 144 blocks.

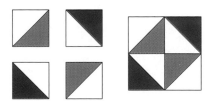

Figure 3
Arrange the triangle/squares to make Block 2.

Quilt Top Assembly
Step 1. Arrange the pieced blocks in 18 rows of 16 blocks each, alternating Blocks 1 and 2, referring to the Placement Diagram for arrangement of blocks.

Step 2. Join blocks in rows; press. Join rows; press.

Finishing

Step 1. Prepare pieced top for tying referring to Chapter 5.

Step 2. Quilt or tie layers together as desired.

Step 3. When quilting or tying is complete, trim batting 1" larger than quilt top all around. Cut backing piece 2 1/4" larger than quilt top all around.

Step 4. Turn edge of backing under 1/4" all around; press. Turn backing to front over batting edge onto quilt top. Machine-stitch through all layers to finish edge.

—By Sandra L. Hatch

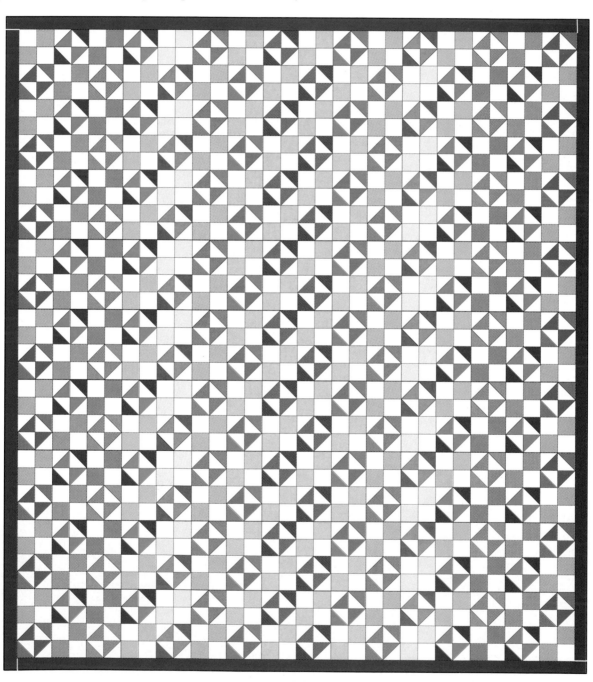

Four-Patch Twist
Placement Diagram
66" x 74"

Glorious Scrap Quilts

Exploding Star

This design is an original arrangement of an old quilt design called Split Square and sometimes referred to as Light and Dark. It dates from before 1880. The basis for the design stems from the contrast between the light and dark fabrics used in each square. You must be brutal when weeding out your medium scraps from the lights and darks! Too many mediums will blend the light and dark areas together, losing the star design.

PROJECT SPECIFICATIONS
Skill Level: Beginner
Project Size: 45 1/2" x 45 1/2"
Block Size: 1 5/8" x 1 5/8"

MATERIALS
- 1 3/4 yards total light scraps or 376 assorted light scrap pieces 2 1/2" square
- 2 yards total dark scraps or 408 assorted dark scrap pieces 2 1/2" square
- Backing 50" x 50"
- Batting 50" x 50"
- Neutral color all-purpose thread
- 5 1/2 yards self-made or purchased binding
- Basic sewing supplies and tools and heavy acrylic or rubber template material

INSTRUCTIONS
Step 1. Make a 2 1/2" x 2 1/2" square template from the rubber or acrylic template material.

Step 2. Cut 376 assorted light squares 2 1/2" x 2 1/2" using template and a rotary cutter. Repeat for 408 assorted dark squares.

Step 3. Place two squares right sides together to make 94 light-light combination pairs, 110 dark-dark combination pairs and 188 light-dark combination pairs as shown in Figure 1.

94 light-light pairs   110 dark-dark pairs   188 light-dark pairs

Figure 1
Place squares right sides together to make pairs as shown.

Step 4. Mark the diagonal line on the wrong side of one square in each pair as shown in Figure 2.

Step 5. Sew each pair together 1/4" away from each side of the diagonal line as shown in Figure 3.

Figure 2
Mark the diagonal on the wrong side of 1 square in each pair as shown.

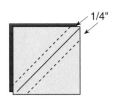

1/4"

Figure 3
Sew each pair together 1/4" away from each side of the diagonal line as shown.

Step 6. Cut each pair apart on the diagonal line as shown in Figure 4 to make 188 light-light right-triangle squares, 220 dark-dark right-triangle squares and 376 light-dark right-triangle squares.

Figure 4
Cut each pair apart on the diagonal line to make right-triangle squares as shown.

Step 7. Press each square open with seams toward the dark fabric on the light-dark squares.

Step 8. Piece 16 blocks as shown in Figure 5. Piece each block with seven horizontal rows made up of seven right-triangle squares. ***Note: Be very careful to lay out each row with the correct square combinations and with each square's seam positioned correctly before sewing.***

Step 9. Press the seams in each odd-numbered row toward the right (R); press the seams in each even-numbered row toward the left (L) as indicated on one side of the piecing diagram in Figure 5. ***Note: It is important to follow all pressing instructions to ensure that the rows and, later, the strips fit together easily.***

	Strip 1	Strip 2	Strip 3	Strip 4	Row

Figure 5
Arrange the stitched pieces as shown. Press seams to
the right (R) or left (L) as indicated.

Block 1, Block 5, Block 9, Block 13
Block 2, Block 6, Block 10, Block 14
Block 3, Block 7, Block 11, Block 15
Block 4, Block 8, Block 12, Block 16

Step 10. Combine Blocks 1–4 to make Strip 1; press all seams down between rows in this strip. Combine Blocks 5–8 to make Strip 2; press all seams up. Combine Blocks 9–12 to make Strip 3; press all seams down. Combine Blocks 13–16 to make Strip 4; press all seams up.

Step 11. Sew Strip 1 to Strip 2 to make one half of the quilt top referring to the Placement Diagram. Sew Strip 3 to Strip 4 to make the second half of the quilt top. Sew the two halves together to complete the top.

Step 12. Mark the top for quilting as desired referring to Chapter 5. The sample quilt was quilted in the ditch of the seams around the light areas.

Step 13. Finish as desired referring to Chapter 5.

—By Sue Harvey

Exploding Star
Placement Diagram
45 1/2" x 45 1/2"

Dresden Star

The Dresden Plate design has been made more complicated in this pretty scrap quilt. Every fan blade uses a different fabric and is emphasized by a repeat of the fabric in points surrounding the center design. Here is a challenge for all quilters whether you choose to hand- or machine-piece the quilt. Whatever your choice, using scraps to create such a beauty will be exciting.

PROJECT SPECIFICATIONS
Skill Level: Experienced
Quilt Size: 90" x 106"
Block Size: 16" x 16"
Number of Blocks Needed: 20

MATERIALS
- 2 1/2 yards each light, medium and dark scraps
- 3 1/2 yards red print
- 7 1/2 yards muslin
- Backing 94" x 110"
- Batting 94" x 110"
- 2 spools off-white all-purpose thread
- 1 spool quilting thread
- 11 1/2 yards self-made or purchased binding
- Basic sewing and quilting supplies

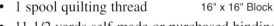

Dresden Star
16" x 16" Block

INSTRUCTIONS
Note: A 1/4" seam allowance is used throughout.

Making Blocks
Step 1. Prepare templates using pattern pieces given. Cut as directed on each piece for one block (whole quilt), choosing light, medium and dark scraps.

Step 2. To piece one block, arrange the B pieces on a flat surface, alternating light, medium and dark

Figure 1
Arrange B pieces in a circle, alternating
light, medium and dark fabrics.

colors, referring to Figure 1, the Placement Diagram and the photo for suggestions.

Step 3. Referring to Figure 2, sew three B pieces together for center; set in C. Join two D pieces with E. *Note: Use the same fabric for D pieces as the B piece to which it will be sewn.* Set the D-E-D unit onto B unit, joining all D-E units with muslin E pieces between.

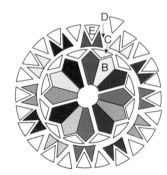

Figure 2
Join pieces as shown, setting in pieces
as needed. Match fabrics used for B
and D in units as shown.

Step 4. Sew F pieces to outside to complete one block. Repeat for 20 blocks.

Step 5. Cut heart pieces, adding a 1/4" seam allowance when cutting. Pin a heart to each corner of each block; appliqué in place by hand or machine using your favorite method.

Assembly
Step 1. Arrange the blocks in five rows of four blocks each; join in rows; press. Join the rows; press.

Step 2. Cut two strips red print 4" x 71 1/2" and two strips 4" x 87 1/2". Sew the short strips to the top and bottom and long strips to sides, mitering corners; press seams toward strips.

Step 3. Cut two strips muslin 10" x 71 1/2" and two strips 10" x 106 1/2". Sew the short strips to the top and bottom and long strips to sides. Press seams toward strips.

Step 4. Arrange eight hearts on each side strip and four hearts across bottom strip, beginning first heart on each side approximately 20" from the top. *Note: If you prefer to place hearts all the way around quilt top, cut more hearts and arrange as desired.*

Step 5. Appliqué hearts in place by hand or machine using your favorite appliqué method.

Finishing

Step 1. Prepare pieced top for quilting referring to Chapter 5.

Step 2. Mark heart designs in border using a water-erasable marker or pencil and the heart pattern given for appliqué.

Step 3. Quilt in the ditch of the seams of the blocks, on marked lines and as desired on borders.

Step 4. When quilting is complete, prepare quilt for binding and finish edges referring to Chapter 5.

—By Bonnie Gheesling

Dresden Star
Placement Diagram
90" x 106"

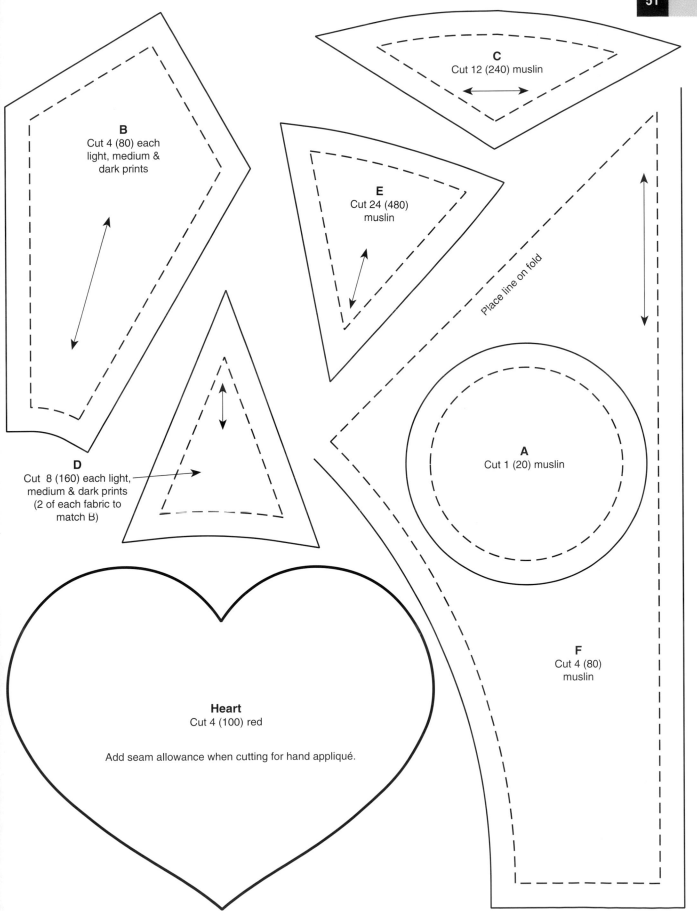

B
Cut 4 (80) each
light, medium &
dark prints

C
Cut 12 (240) muslin

E
Cut 24 (480)
muslin

Place line on fold

D
Cut 8 (160) each light,
medium & dark prints
(2 of each fabric to
match B)

A
Cut 1 (20) muslin

F
Cut 4 (80)
muslin

Heart
Cut 4 (100) red

Add seam allowance when cutting for hand appliqué.

Indian Summer

Fall colors are easy to find in most any scrap collection. Tie these scraps together with a background print to make this quick and easy wall quilt.

PROJECT SPECIFICATIONS

Skill Level: Beginner

Quilt Size: 41" x 59"

Block Size: 18" x 18"

Number of Blocks Needed: 6

MATERIALS

- 1 1/8 yards dark red print for block centers, border and binding
- 1 1/2 yards beige or tan tone-on-tone for background
- 1/8 yard each of 10 prints in fall colors
- Backing 45" x 63"
- Batting 45" x 63"
- 6 1/2 yards self-made or purchased binding
- Neutral color all-purpose thread
- 1 spool quilting thread
- Basic sewing and quilting supplies

Pinwheel
18" x 18"

INSTRUCTIONS

Note: A 1/4" seam allowance is used throughout.

Cutting

Step 1. Cut a 6 7/8" by fabric width strip of background fabric. Cut the strip into six 6 7/8" segments. Cut each square segment in half on the diagonal. Repeat with a red print strip.

Step 2. Cut eight strips background fabric 3 7/8" by fabric width. Cut into eighty-four 3 7/8" segments. Cut each square segment in half on the diagonal.

Step 3. Cut two strips background fabric 3 1/2" by fabric width. Cut into twenty-four 3 1/2" segments.

Step 4. Cut six 3 7/8" x 3 7/8" squares from each of the 10 fall prints. Cut each square in half on the diagonal.

Piecing Blocks

Step 1. Sew fall print triangle to background triangle as shown in Figure 1. Repeat for all 120 fall print triangles. Press seams toward darker fabric.

Indian Summer
Placement Diagram
41" x 59"

Step 2. Separate pieced squares into six sets, one for each block, with two of each fabric in a set.

Step 3. Arrange one set with two each of the red and background triangles cut from the 6 7/8" squares, four 3 1/2" background squares and eight background triangles cut from the 3 7/8" squares. (Refer to Figure 2.)

Figure 1
Sew a fall print triangle to a background triangle.

Figure 2
Arrange the pieced sets with the background squares and triangles as shown.

Step 4. Referring again to Figure 2, join the pieces to make four units; press. Join the units to complete one block; press. Repeat for six blocks.

Quilt Top Assembly
Step 1. Lay out the six blocks on a flat surface. Alternate the blocks so the placement of the large triangles in the centers alternate referring to the Placement Diagram.

Step 2. Join blocks in rows; press. Join rows; press.

Step 3. Cut two strips dark red 3" x 36 1/2". Sew a strip to the top and bottom; press seams toward

strips. Cut two more strips 3" x 59 1/2". Sew a strip to each side; press seams toward strips.

Finishing
Step 1. Prepare pieced top for quilting referring to Chapter 5.

Step 2. Quilt in the ditch of the seams of the blocks and as desired on borders by hand or machine.

Step 3. When quilting is complete, finish edges referring to Chapter 5.

—By Lucy A. Fazely

Happy Scrappy Lap Quilt

I challenged myself to use only scraps I had on hand to construct a quilt from one of my favorite quilt designs. The result is a simple quilt bursting with color and character. Large pieces which make assembly quick and easy are an added plus. If you like this design, construct more blocks to create a larger wall quilt or bed-size quilt.

PROJECT SPECIFICATIONS
Skill Level: Intermediate
Quilt Size: 46" x 46"
Block Size: 12" x 12"

MATERIALS
- 1 3/4 yards total assorted blue, green and red scraps
- 1 1/2 yards blue paisley print
- 3/4 yard cream-on-cream print
- Backing 50" x 50"
- Batting 50" x 50"
- Neutral color all-purpose thread
- 5 1/4 yards self-made or purchased binding

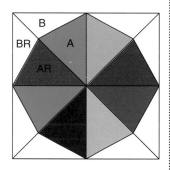

Happy Scrappy
12" x 12" Block

INSTRUCTIONS
Note: A 1/4" seam allowance is used throughout.

Making Blocks
Step 1. Trace patterns onto cardboard or plastic. Cut fabric pieces as directed on pattern pieces.

Step 2. Sew A to B; press seam toward the scrap piece. Sew AR to BR; press seams toward cream-on-cream piece. Sew the A-B unit to the AR-BR unit to make a wedge as shown in Figure 1. Repeat to make wedges from all pieces.

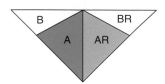

Figure 1
Join the A-B unit to the
AR-BR unit as shown.

Step 3. Set aside four wedges for corners. Sew four sets of two wedges to make side blocks as shown in Figure 2.

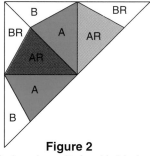

Figure 2
Join 2 wedge units for side blocks.

Step 4. Stitch four wedges together to complete one block as shown in Figure 3; repeat for five blocks.

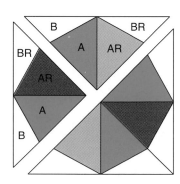

Figure 3
Join 4 wedges to complete 1 block.

Assembly
Step 1. Cut eight pieces blue paisley 3" x 12 1/2". Join strips with blocks as shown in Figure 4; press seams toward strips. Cut two pieces blue paisley 3" x 17 1/2". Join one with the top right corner block and one with the bottom left corner block, again referring to Figure 4.

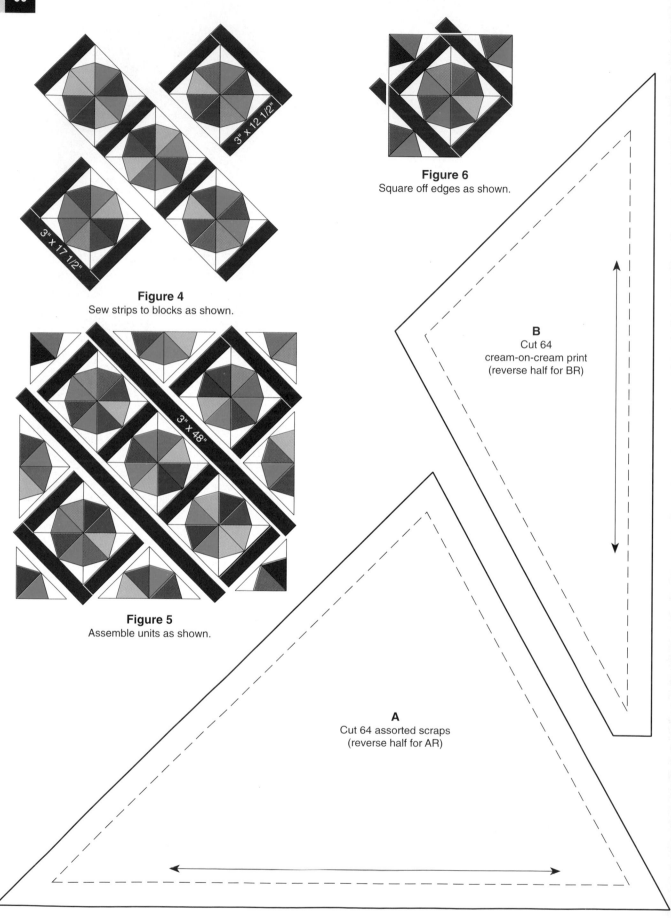

Figure 4
Sew strips to blocks as shown.

3" x 12 1/2"

3" x 17 1/2"

Figure 5
Assemble units as shown.

3" x 48"

Figure 6
Square off edges as shown.

B
Cut 64
cream-on-cream print
(reverse half for BR)

A
Cut 64 assorted scraps
(reverse half for AR)

Step 2. Cut two strips 3" x 48" blue paisley. Arrange these strips with the sashed sections and side and corner blocks referring to Figure 5. Join the units to complete the pieced center. *Note: The blue paisley strips are cut longer than necessary to allow for cutting them at an angle at the sides when piecing is complete.*

Step 3. Press the assembled center; trim excess paisley strips even with block edges to square up center as shown in Figure 6. It should measure 41 1/2" x 41 1/2", including seams.

Step 4. Cut two strips blue paisley 3" x 41 1/2"; sew to opposite sides; press seams toward strips. Cut two more strips 3" x 46 1/2"; sew to top and bottom; press seams toward strips.

Finishing
Step 1. Finish as directed in Chapter 5, using self-made or purchased binding for edges.

—By Holly Daniels

Happy Scrappy Lap Quilt
Placement Diagram
46" x 46"

My Family Valentines

When you walk through the front door of my home, you face a wall that is always dressed in a quilt. In 1995 as Valentine's Day approached and, with it, my turn to host the small quilt group to which I belong, I had not one but two good reasons to design and make a heart quilt to display in my entryway.

As I worked on the design I knew I wanted the quilt to be informal and homey so a scrap quilt seemed the perfect choice. I included four heart blocks—each representing one family member.

These blocks were constructed in a Log Cabin fashion. Instead of quilting the piece I used 242 buttons to tie the quilt layers together. Most of the buttons came from the button box my sister-in-law gave me many years ago. When my husband, son and daughter asked, "Which heart is mine?" I responded with, "Which do you think is yours?" Amazingly, each one selected the heart made with him/her in mind!

QUILT SPECIFICATIONS
Skill Level: Intermediate

Quilt Size: 35" x 35"

Block Size: 8 1/2" x 8 1/2" unframed;
    10 1/4" x 10 1/4" framed

MATERIALS
- 1 yard black-and-white plaid
- 1/8 yard each 25 fabrics in red, pink, blue, lavender, black-and-white prints, etc., or scraps (see list in Step 1 under Cutting for scrap sizes)
- 1/4 yard each of 4 neutral prints
- 1/4 yard red-and-black check
- 1/2 yard red-and-black print
- Matching all-purpose thread
- 1 spool neutral quilting thread
- Backing 38" x 38"
- Batting 38" x 38"
- 240 buttons
- Embroidery floss in various colors
- 4 1/4 yards self-made or purchased binding

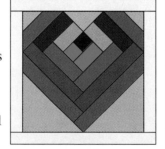

Heart Block
8 1/2" x 8 1/2" without frames
10 1/4" x 10 1/4" with frames

- Basic sewing supplies, template plastic, rotary cutter, mat and ruler

Cutting
Step 1. Cut four strips 1 1/2" x 17" red or pink fabric or scraps (fabric 1). Cut the following lengths of 1 1/2"-wide strips from any suggested color: four strips 20" long (fabric 2); four strips 21" long (fabric 3); three strips 24" long (fabric 4); four strips 23" long (fabric 5); three strips 28" long (fabric 6); and three strips 39" long (fabric 7).

Step 2. From the length of black-and-white plaid cut two strips 2" x 28 1/2" (AA). Refold fabric selvage to selvage and from the width cut two strips 2" x 28 1/2" (BB) and one strip 10 3/4" by fabric width. From this strip cut six 3"-wide segments (CC) lengthwise and three strips 3" by remaining width as shown in Figure 1. From these strips, cut six 3" x 10 3/4" segments for DD. *Note: CC and DD are the same size but the grain goes in different directions. This is not absolutely necessary. If you prefer, cut 12 strips 3" x 10 3/4" on either the crosswise or lengthwise grain.*

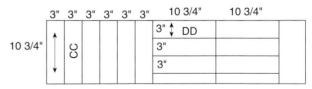

Figure 1
Cut pieces for CC and DD as shown.

Step 3. Cut one strip plaid 1 1/2" by fabric width (heart units C and D for use as a strip in one block and on the multicolored border). Refer to Figure 9 for placement later. *Note: The black-and-white plaid used on the quilt shown is longer than it is wide. When making this quilt the plaid was cut so that all the borders have the longer part of the plaid going in the same direction. If your plaid does not have this difference, cut all strips across width of fabric.*

Step 4. For each heart block, cut lettered pieces from fabrics 1–7 in the following sizes referring to Figure 2: A—1 1/2" x 1 1/2"; B—1 1/2" x 2 1/2"; C—1 1/2" x 3 1/2"; D—1 1/2" x 4 1/2"; E—1 1/2" x 5 1/2"; and F—1 1/2" x 6 1/2". For pieces G, H and I, cut 1 1/2" strips and use templates given to cut pieces from each strip. *Note: If using the 1/8 yard purchased fabric, each heart uses seven different fabrics (28 fabrics for four hearts). Except for the center A square, each fabric is used in at least two of the logs of the heart. Figure 2 illustrates the placement of each of the seven fabrics.*

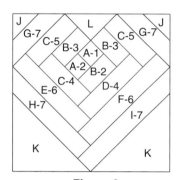

Figure 2
The drawing shows order of piecing and suggested fabric use by number.

Step 5. Cut the remaining yardage from the 25 fabrics into 1 1/2"-wide across fabric width strips for border segments.

Step 6. From each of the 1/4-yard neutral pieces cut one strip 1 3/8" by fabric width. From this strip cut two pieces 1 3/8" x 9" for M and two strips 1 3/8" x 10 3/4" for N. Cut two each J and K triangles. Cut one L triangle.

Step 7. From red-and-black check cut four squares 4" x 4" (EE), five squares 3" x 3" (FF) and one strip 1 1/2" x 13" (for heart units E and F in only one block).

Step 8. From the red-and-black print cut four squares 3" x 3" (GG) and one strip 1 1/2" x 24" (for heart units G, H and I). Use this fabric to create self-made binding for finishing the quilt edge.

Piecing Blocks
Note: To simplify piecing, each log of the heart is identified with a letter and a number. The letter stands for the unit and the number for the fabric. For example, A-1 is unit A, heart fabric 1.

Step 1. Join A-1 to A-2; press seam to A-1. Turn so

A-1 is on top and A-2 is below A-1 as shown in Figure 3.

Figure 3
Join A-1 and A-2; turn so A-1 is on top of A-2.

Figure 4
Turn so A pieces are on top of B-2.

Step 2. Place B-2 on top of the A unit, right sides together; stitch. Press seam to B-2. Turn so A-2/A-1 are on top of B-2 as shown in Figure 4.

Step 3. Place B-3 on top of right side of the above unit, right sides together; stitch leaving 1/4" seam allowance free as shown in Figure 5; backstitch to secure. Press seam to B-3 as shown in Figure 6.

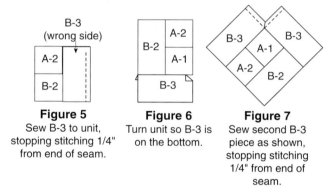

Figure 5
Sew B-3 to unit, stopping stitching 1/4" from end of seam.

Figure 6
Turn unit so B-3 is on the bottom.

Figure 7
Sew second B-3 piece as shown, stopping stitching 1/4" from end of seam.

Step 4. Place second B-3 on top of A-2/A-1 with right sides together; stitch leaving 1/4" seam allowance free as shown in Figure 7; backstitch to secure. Press seam to B-3.

Step 5. Referring to Figure 2 and sequence given, continue adding additional logs in this manner until the heart is complete, leaving no other seam allowances free. Stitching sequence continues: C-4, D-4, C-5, C-5, E-6, F-6, G-7, G-7, H-7 and I-7.

Step 6. Referring to Figure 8, stitch K and J to the respective corners. Set in L; press seam toward the heart.

Step 7. Stitch 1 3/8" x 9" M pieces to opposite sides of heart block; press seams toward strips. Stitch 1 3/8" x 10 3/4" N pieces to top and bottom; press seams toward strips. Repeat for four blocks.

Border Assembly
Step 1. Using remaining 26 strips of heart fabrics (25 scraps and one black-and-white plaid), stitch all lengths together. Press all seams in one direction.

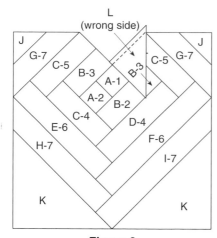

Figure 8
Sew J and K corner triangles to square; set in L.

Step 2. Cut four 2 1/2" segments from the pieced strip to make multicolored border strips as shown in Figure 9. Each strip is short two 1 1/2" x 2 1/2" segments. From the remaining strips fabric cut eight more 1 1/2" x 2 1/2" units. Sew one of these to each of the four long border segments as shown in Figure 10. *Note: Each multicolored border strip should have twenty-eight 1 1/2" x 2 1/2" units.*

Quilt Top Assembly
Step 1. Referring to photo and Placement Diagram, determine heart block placement. Lay out other fabric sections and borders referring to Figure 11.

My Family Valentines
Placement Diagram
35" x 35"

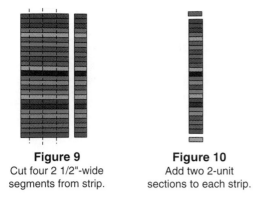

Figure 9
Cut four 2 1/2"-wide
segments from strip.

Figure 10
Add two 2-unit
sections to each strip.

Step 2. Sew two horizontal rows using pieces FF, DD, GG, DD and FF referring to Figure 11. Press seams toward FF and GG.

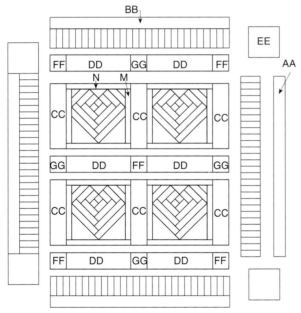

Figure 11
Arrange blocks with cut pieces as shown.

Step 3. Sew two horizontal rows using pieces CC and heart blocks; press seams toward blocks.

Step 4. Sew an AA strip to a multicolored border strip; repeat for second AA strip. Sew a BB strip to the remaining multicolored border strips referring to Figure 11.

Step 5. Sew an EE unit to the top and bottom of both AA/multicolored borders.

Step 6. Arrange all rows and borders referring to Figure 11; join to complete quilt top; press.

Finishing

Step 1. Sandwich batting between completed top and prepared backing piece. Pin layers together to hold flat.

Step 2. Place buttons as illustrated by red dots on Figure 12. Using 3–6 strands of matching embroidery floss, sew buttons in place as desired.

Step 3. Quilt in the border strips as illustrated by blue dotted lines in Figure 12.

Step 4. Trim excess backing and batting even with quilt top. Finish edges with self-made binding using red-and-black print referring to Chapter 5 for instructions.

—By Sherry Reis

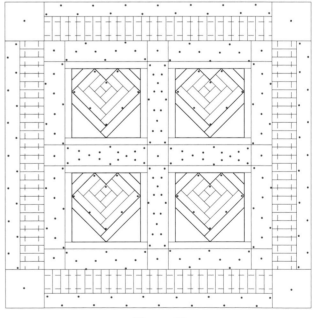

Figure 12
Sew buttons where marked by red dots.
Quilt using blue dotted line as a guide.

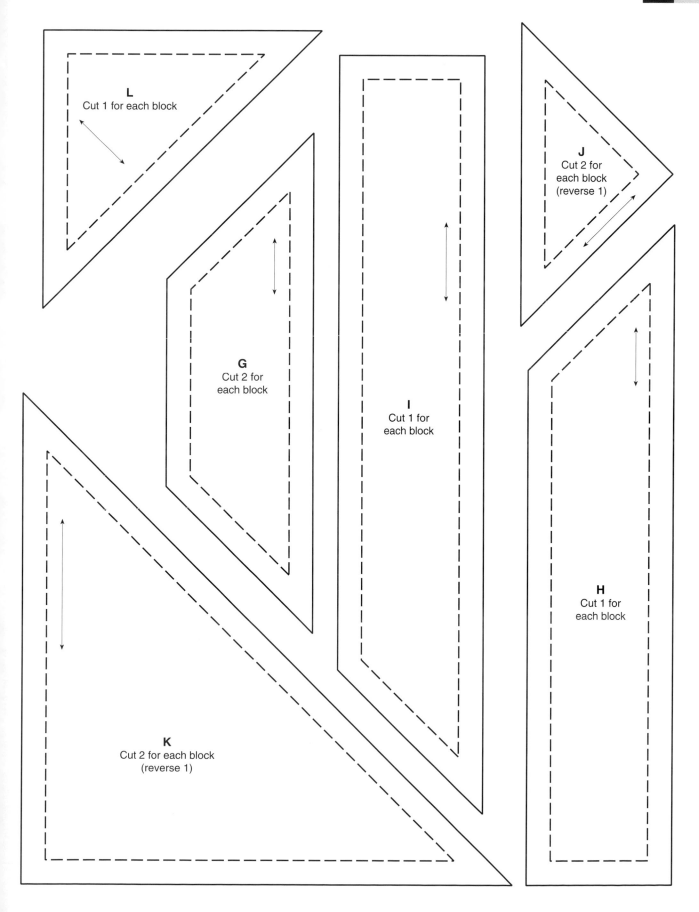

L
Cut 1 for each block

J
Cut 2 for
each block
(reverse 1)

G
Cut 2 for
each block

I
Cut 1 for
each block

H
Cut 1 for
each block

K
Cut 2 for each block
(reverse 1)

Quilted With Love

Use country blue and rose prints or a color scheme to match your decor.
This glorious miniature scrap quilt will win its way into everyone's heart.

QUILT SPECIFICATIONS
Skill Level: Beginner
Quilt Size: 17" x 17"
Block Size: 2" x 2"
Number of Blocks: 25

MATERIALS
- 1/8 yard cream-on-cream print
- Scraps of pink and blue prints
- 1/2 yard medium blue print
- 1/4 yard cream floral print
- Batting 19" x 19"
- Matching all-purpose thread
- 1 spool contrasting quilting thread
- Basic sewing supplies, template plastic, rotary cutter, mat and ruler

Assembly

Step 1. Layer pink and blue prints in 13 pairs with right sides together. Cut one 3 1/4" x 3 1/4" square from each pair. Cut each square across both diagonals to make four triangles as shown in Figure 1.

Step 2. Sew each triangle set together beginning at the squared corner; press seams toward blue fabric. Mix joined half-square triangles into different combinations; stitch together to form squares as shown in Figure 2. Repeat for 13 squares.

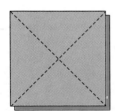
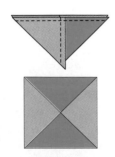

Figure 1
Cut squares twice on the diagonal to make 4 triangles from each square.

Figure 2
Stitch 2 triangle sections together make a square as shown.

Step 3. Cut 12 squares cream-on-cream print 2 1/2" x 2 1/2".

Step 4. Trace heart shape onto template plastic. Trace one heart onto the right side of blue and pink fabrics; cut six hearts from each color family. Cut out shape, leaving a scant 1/4" seam allowance.

Step 5. Clip seam almost to traced line at inside angle at top corner of each heart. Carefully fold seam allowance back all around traced line; baste near fold. Position a heart in the center of each cream square. Appliqué in place by hand using matching thread.

Step 6. Arrange appliquéd heart squares in rows with pieced squares referring to Figure 3, placing pink and blue hearts as shown in the photo and Placement Diagram. Join in rows; press. Join the rows to complete the pieced center; press.

Figure 3
Arrange blocks in rows.

Step 7. Cut backing piece from medium blue print 20" x 20"; set aside. From the remaining medium blue print, cut two strips 1" x 10 1/2"; sew a strip to opposite sides; press. Cut two more strips 1" x 11 1/2"; sew to top and bottom; press.

Step 8. Cut two strips cream floral 3 1/2" x 11 1/2"; sew a strip to opposite sides. Cut two more strips 3 1/2" x 17 1/2"; sew to top and bottom; press.

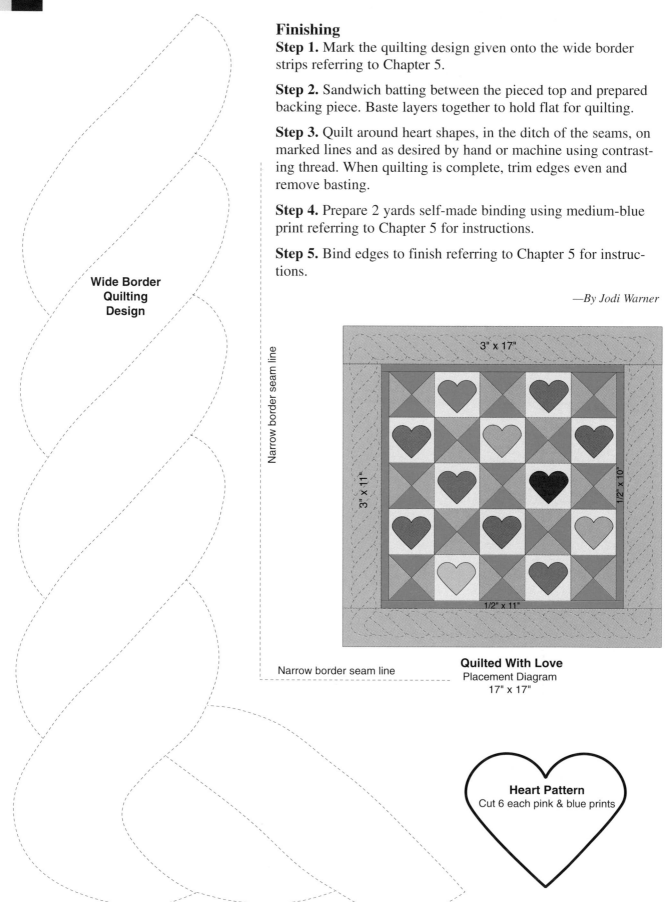

**Wide Border
Quilting
Design**

Narrow border seam line

Narrow border seam line

Finishing

Step 1. Mark the quilting design given onto the wide border strips referring to Chapter 5.

Step 2. Sandwich batting between the pieced top and prepared backing piece. Baste layers together to hold flat for quilting.

Step 3. Quilt around heart shapes, in the ditch of the seams, on marked lines and as desired by hand or machine using contrasting thread. When quilting is complete, trim edges even and remove basting.

Step 4. Prepare 2 yards self-made binding using medium-blue print referring to Chapter 5 for instructions.

Step 5. Bind edges to finish referring to Chapter 5 for instructions.

—By Jodi Warner

3" x 17"

3" x 11"

1/2" x 10"

1/2" x 11"

Quilted With Love
Placement Diagram
17" x 17"

Heart Pattern
Cut 6 each pink & blue prints

Quilting the Web!

These days, every magazine and newspaper seems to be full of news about the Internet. The most colorful aspect of this global network is the World Wide Web. Those of you who are on-line know how much fun it is to search the Web for interesting information. You'll also discover a number of quilters with home pages on the Web. This quilt reminds me of the Web, which has structure, but still has plenty of surprises.

PROJECT SPECIFICATIONS
Skill Level: Intermediate
Project Size: 48" x 48"
Block Size: 12" x 12"

MATERIALS
- Scraps totaling 1 yard for each color value in light, medium and dark
- Backing 52" x 52"
- Batting 52" x 52"
- 6 yards self-made or purchased binding
- Basic sewing supplies and tools, template plastic, chalk pencil or fade-out pen and tracing paper

Quilting the Web!
12" x 12" Block

INSTRUCTIONS
Step 1. Prepare templates using pattern pieces given. Cut as directed on each piece.

Step 2. To piece one block, sew five dark A pieces together. Sew two medium A's together twice. Sew medium and dark C's and CRs to B as shown in Figure 1.

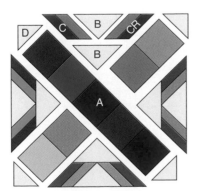

Figure 1
Sew pieces together as shown to make 1 block.

Step 3. Sew B to one end of one C-B unit; repeat for four units. Sew a C-B unit to each side of a medium A-A unit; repeat. Sew the A-B-C units to the strip of dark A's and D pieces to the corners to complete one block; press. Repeat for 16 blocks, varying the colors as much as possible.

Step 4. Arrange blocks in four rows of four blocks each referring to the Placement Diagram. Join the blocks in rows; press. Join the rows to complete the top; press.

Step 5. Prepare top for quilting and finish referring to Chapter 5. ***Note:*** *The sample quilt was machine-quilted in the ditch of some seams.*

—*By Connie Rand*

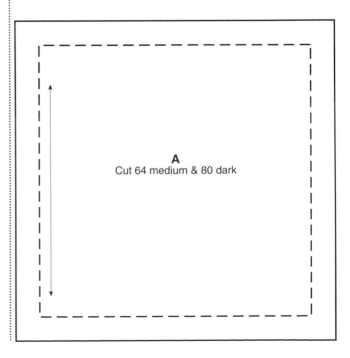

A
Cut 64 medium & 80 dark

Quilting the Web!
Placement Diagram
48" x 48"

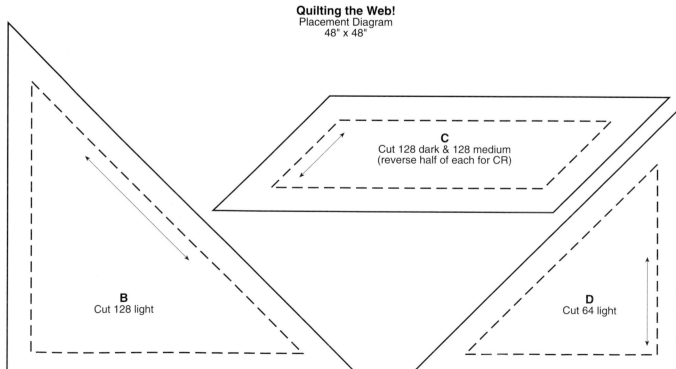

C
Cut 128 dark & 128 medium
(reverse half of each for CR)

B
Cut 128 light

D
Cut 64 light

Scrap Quilting Made Easy

Miniature Fan Quilt

A beginner can create this pretty little quilt with little trouble. Change the colors to make a seasonal wall quilt or to match a specific color scheme. The pieces are small so coordinated scraps can be used.

QUILT SPECIFICATIONS
Skill Level: Beginner
Quilt Size: Approximately 18 1/2" x 18 1/2"
Block Size: 4" x 4"
Number of Blocks: 13

MATERIALS
- 2/3 yard paisley print for background
- 9" x 9" square each dark and medium peach
- 6" x 6" square medium blue
- 1 fat quarter each light and dark blue
- 6" x 12" piece brown print
- All-purpose threads to match fabrics
- 1 spool white quilting thread
- Backing 22" x 22"
- Batting 22" x 22"
- 8" x 24" piece medium blue binding fabric for straight-edge binding
- Basic sewing supplies and 1/4" bias bar strip

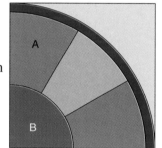

Fan Block
4" x 4"

INSTRUCTIONS
Cutting
Step 1. Prepare templates using pattern pieces given. Cut as directed on each piece.

Step 2. Cut nine squares light blue 4 1/2" x 4 1/2" and two strips each 1" x 12 1/2" and 1" x 13 1/2".

Step 3. Cut nine bias strips from dark blue 1" x 6 1/2".

Assembly
Step 1. To complete one block, sew A pieces together placing a dark peach A between two paisley A's; press. Repeat for nine units using this color combination.

Step 2. Pin one of these A units on a light blue square matching side seams as shown in Figure 1;

repeat for the nine A units. Baste along top curved edge; do not turn edge under.

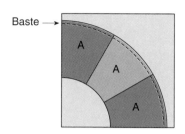

Figure 1
Place stitched A unit on background square.

Step 3. Appliqué brown print B pieces to bottom curved edge, turning under the curved seam 1/4".

Step 4. Using a bias bar strip, sew the nine dark blue bias strips. ***Note: If you do not have a bias bar strip, create 1/4"-wide (finished size) bias strips using your favorite method.*** Appliqué a strip to the top edge of each fan unit; press.

Step 5. Arrange nine blocks in three rows of three blocks each; join in rows. Join the rows; press.

Step 6. Sew 1" x 12 1/2" light blue strips to opposite sides of pieced center; press seams toward strips. Sew 1" x 13 1/2" light blue strips to remaining sides; press seams toward strips.

Step 7. Cut two squares paisley print 10 1/8" x 10 1/8". Cut each square once on the diagonal to create the corner triangles.

Step 8. Sew a triangle to each corner of the pieced center; press seams toward triangles.

Step 9. Sew a medium blue A between two light peach A's; repeat for four units. Set a dark blue B in at the corners. Appliqué one of these fan units on the corner of each paisley triangle referring to the Placement Diagram and photo.

Finishing
Step 1. Prepare quilt top for quilting referring to instructions on page Chapter 5.

Step 2. Quilt in the ditch of seams and as desired by hand or machine using white quilting thread.

Step 3. Prepare 2 1/8 yards straight-edge binding from 8" x 24" piece medium blue binding fabric and finish edges referring to Chapter 5.

—By Joyce Mori

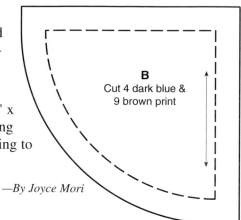

B
Cut 4 dark blue & 9 brown print

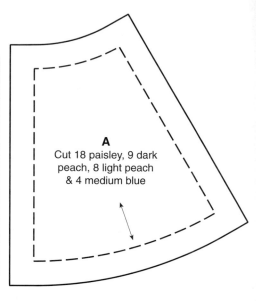

A
Cut 18 paisley, 9 dark peach, 8 light peach & 4 medium blue

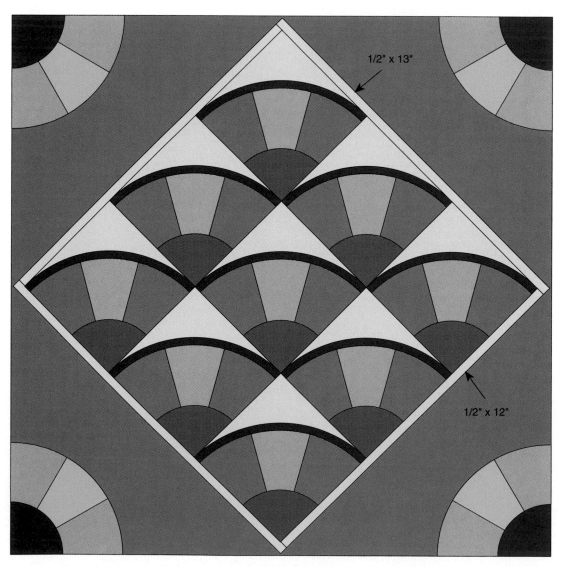

1/2" x 13"

1/2" x 12"

Miniature Fan Quilt
Placement Diagram
Approximately 18 1/2" x 18 1/2"

Scrap Quilting Made Easy

Diamonds Jubilee

This scrap quilt is best pieced with lots and lots of color.
Although it looks random, the colors have been very carefully chosen and
placed to bounce off each other, giving the quilt a feeling of movement.
Plan carefully so that each color is evenly sprinkled throughout the quilt.

PROJECT SPECIFICATIONS
Skill Level: Intermediate
Quilt Size: 90" x 90"

MATERIALS
- 5 yards white for back-ground and borders
- 4 1/2 yards total of various scraps of several different colored fabrics
- Backing 94" x 94"
- Batting 94" x 94"
- Neutral color all-purpose thread
- 10 1/4 yards self-made or purchased binding
- Basic sewing tools and supplies

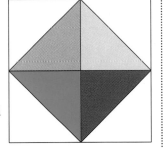

Four-Patch Variation
7" x 7" Block

Diamond Block
7" x 7"

INSTRUCTIONS
Step 1. Cut eight scrap squares 2 1/4" x 2 1/4" and four white rectangles 2 1/4" x 4".

Step 2. Sew four squares together to make a Four-Patch. Sew the remaining 2 1/4" squares to each end of two rectangles. Join these units referring to Figure 1 to make the Four-Patch Variation block; repeat for 60 blocks.

Step 3. Cut four squares scraps and two squares white 4 3/8" x 4 3/8". Cut each square in half on the

diagonal to make triangles. Set aside one triangle of each color for another block.

Step 4. Sew a scrap triangle to a white triangle; repeat for four triangle/squares. Arrange squares with scraps in the center. Sew to complete one Diamond Block as shown in Figure 2; repeat for 61 blocks.

Step 5. Cut four scrap and two white squares 2 1/4" x 2 1/4". Cut one white 2 1/4" x 4" rectangle. Join two scrap squares; sew a white square to each end. Sew a scrap square to each end of the white rectangle. Join units to make Half Four-Patch units as shown in Figure 3. Repeat for 24 units.

Step 6. Cut one each white and scrap squares 4 3/8" x 4 3/8". Cut each square in half on the diagonal to make triangles. Sew a white triangle to a scrap triangle twice. Join to make Half Edge units as shown in Figure 4. Repeat for 20 units.

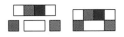

Figure 3
Join pieces to make Half Four-Patch units; make 24 units.

Figure 4
Join pieces to make Half Edge units; make 20 units.

Step 7. Cut two each white and scrap squares 4 3/8" x 4 3/8". Cut each square in half on the diagonal to make triangles. Sew a white triangle to a scrap triangle; repeat for four units. These will be used on the corners of the quilt.

Assembly
Step 1. Arrange Half Four-Patch units with Half Edge units and corner squares in a row as shown in

Figure 5
Arrange the Half Four-Patch units with the Half Edge units and corner squares to make a row; make 2 rows.

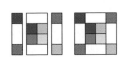

Figure 1
Join pieces to make Four-Patch Variation as shown; make 60 blocks.

Figure 2
Join pieces to make Diamond Block; make 61 blocks.

Figure 5; repeat, turning corner squares as shown.

Step 2. Arrange the Half Four-Patch units with Diamond and Four-Patch Variation blocks as shown in Figure 6; repeat for six rows.

Figure 6
Arrange the Half Four-Patch units with Diamond and Four-Patch Variation blocks to make a row; make 6 rows.

Figure 7
Arrange the Half Edge units with Diamond and Four-Patch Variation blocks to make a row; make 5 rows.

Step 3. Arrange the Half Edge units with Diamond and Four-Patch Variation blocks as shown in Figure 7; repeat for five rows.

Step 4. Arrange rows referring to the Placement Diagram; join rows to complete pieced section.

Step 5. Cut four strips white 3 1/2" x 90 1/2". Sew a strip to each side, mitering corners; press quilt top.

Finishing

Step 1. Sandwich batting between the completed top and prepared backing piece. Baste or pin layers together to hold flat for quilting.

Step 2. Quilt in the ditch of seams by hand or machine and as desired. When quilting is complete, trim edges even.

Step 3. Bind edges using self-made or purchased binding referring to Chapter 5.

—By Judith Anton

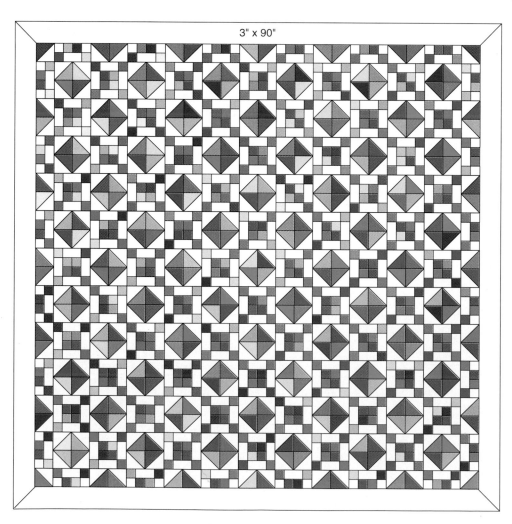

3" x 90"

Diamonds Jubilee
Placement Diagram
90" x 90"

Hmmm

The hummingbird is such a magical little bird. It darts so quickly it can barely be seen flying through the air. Hummingbirds come in a variety of colors and are attracted to many flowers. If you don't have large enough scraps for this coordinated look, using more variety in your fabrics for the hummingbirds and flowers would be very appropriate.

QUILT SPECIFICATIONS

Skill Level: Intermediate
Quilt Size: 29" x 30 1/2"
Block Size: 6" x 6 1/2"
Number of Blocks: 9

MATERIALS

- 1 fat quarter each yellow check and red and green prints
- Scraps brown and yellow prints
- 1/2 yard blue print
- 1/2 yard large floral print
- 1 yard white-on-white print
- All-purpose thread to match fabric
- 1 spool nylon monofilament thread
- Backing 32" x 34"
- Batting 32" x 34"

Flower Block
6" x 6 1/2"

Piecing the Blocks

Step 1. Cut pieces as directed in each chart in Figures 1 and 2 for blocks referring to the Color Key, the photo and Placement Diagram for color suggestions.

Step 2. To piece one Flower block, place a 2" x 2" blue print square on a white-on-white 2" x 3 1/2" rectangle. Sew across the diagonal as shown in Figure 1; repeat on other end. Press back the stitched triangle; trim excess layers if desired. Repeat for three units. Repeat with 3 1/2" x 2 1/2" white-on-white rectangle as in Figure 1.

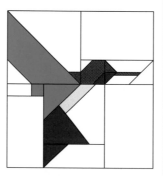

Hummingbird Block
6" x 6 1/2"

Step 3. Arrange the pieced units with the 3 1/2" x 3 1/2" yellow check square and the 2" x 2" white-on-white squares in rows. Join pieces in rows; join rows to complete one block; repeat for five blocks.

Step 4. To make one Hummingbird block, layer and stitch pieces referring to Figure 2 to piece units. Arrange the pieced units to complete one block; repeat for four Hummingbird blocks.

Assembly

Step 1. Arrange the blocks in rows referring to the Placement Diagram. Join in rows; join rows to complete center. Press.

Step 2. Cut two strips white-on-white 2" x 20" and two strips 2" x 21 1/2". Sew short strips to sides and long strips to top and bottom; press seams toward strips.

Step 3. Cut two strips blue print 1 1/2" x 23" and two strips 1 1/2" x 23 1/2". Sew short strips to sides and long strips to top and bottom; press seams toward strips.

Step 4. Cut two strips large floral print 3 1/2" x 25" and two strips 3 1/2" x 29 1/2". Sew short strips to sides and long strips to top and bottom; press seams toward strips.

Finishing

Step 1. Prepare quilt top for quilting referring to Chapter 5.

Step 2. Quilt in the ditch of seams and as desired by machine using monofilament thread in the top of the machine and all-purpose thread to match backing in the bobbin.

Step 3. Prepare 3 1/2 yards self-made binding from large floral print; finish edges referring to Chapter 5.

—By Lisa Christensen

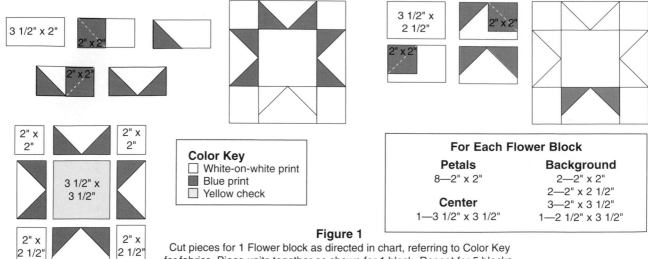

Color Key
- ☐ White-on-white print
- ▨ Blue print
- ☐ Yellow check

For Each Flower Block	
Petals	**Background**
8—2" x 2"	2—2" x 2"
	2—2" x 2 1/2"
Center	3—2" x 3 1/2"
1—3 1/2" x 3 1/2"	1—2 1/2" x 3 1/2"

Figure 1
Cut pieces for 1 Flower block as directed in chart, referring to Color Key for fabrics. Piece units together as shown for 1 block. Repeat for 5 blocks.

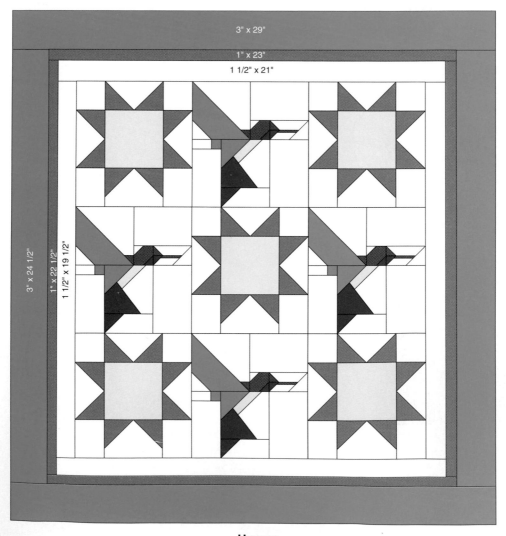

Hmmm
Placement Diagram
29" x 30 1/2"

le Easy

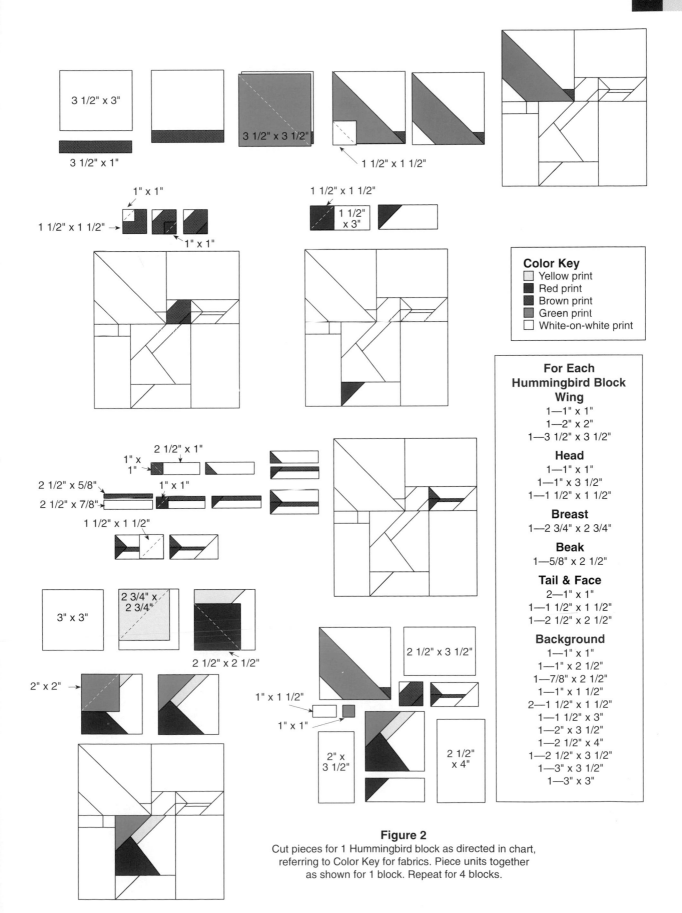

Figure 2
Cut pieces for 1 Hummingbird block as directed in chart,
referring to Color Key for fabrics. Piece units together
as shown for 1 block. Repeat for 4 blocks.

Color Key
Yellow print
Red print
Brown print
Green print
White-on-white print

For Each
Hummingbird Block
Wing
1—1" x 1"
1—2" x 2"
1—3 1/2" x 3 1/2"

Head
1—1" x 1"
1—1" x 3 1/2"
1—1 1/2" x 1 1/2"

Breast
1—2 3/4" x 2 3/4"

Beak
1—5/8" x 2 1/2"

Tail & Face
2—1" x 1"
1—1 1/2" x 1 1/2"
1—2 1/2" x 2 1/2"

Background
1—1" x 1"
1—1" x 2 1/2"
1—7/8" x 2 1/2"
1—1" x 1 1/2"
2—1 1/2" x 1 1/2"
1—1 1/2" x 3"
1—2" x 3 1/2"
1—2 1/2" x 4"
1—2 1/2" x 3 1/2"
1—3" x 3 1/2"
1—3" x 3"

A Happy Scrappy Christmas

Christmas in August

✛

Victorian Mantel Quilt

✛

Folk Art Mantel Quilt

✛

Crazy Patchwork Christmas Vest

✛

Scrap Bag Snail's Trail

✛

Treeflake

✛

String-Quilted Gift Bags

✛

String of Stars

Christmas in August

Nothing is sacred in my house! As my children outgrow their dresses or shirts, I am delighted. Some clothes are immediately dismantled and cut into fabric swatches for a future project. It doesn't take long to have more fabric than places to store it in! I have an endless array of prints, plaids and paisleys, and I know where each one came from. A sleeve here, a uniform blouse there, ties, skirts, jackets—you name it, I have it. I use everything except shoes! Christmas in August is a collection of predominantly red and white fabrics mixed with some greens.

PROJECT SPECIFICATIONS

Skill Level: Beginner

Quilt Size: 47" x 50 1/2"

Block Size: 3 1/2" x 3 1/2"

Number of Blocks: 156

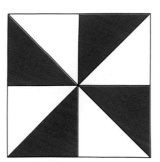

Pinwheel
3 1/2" x 3 1/2" Block

MATERIALS

- 2 yards total of assorted medium dark to dark prints
- 2 yards total of assorted light to white prints
- 1/2 yard total of assorted red or Christmas prints
- 1/2 yard total of assorted green prints
- 1 1/2 yards red print or solid for borders
- Backing 51" x 54"
- Batting 51" x 54"
- 6 yards self-made or purchased binding
- Neutral color all-purpose thread
- 1 spool quilting thread
- Basic sewing and quilting supplies

INSTRUCTIONS

Note: A 1/4" seam allowance is used throughout.

Piecing Blocks

Step 1. Cut fabric scraps into 2 5/8" x 2 5/8" squares. You will need two squares each of a dark and a light fabric for each block. Place a light square on top of a dark square with right sides together. Draw a line on the diagonal.

Step 2. Sew a 1/4" seam on each side of the line as shown in Figure 1. Cut pieces apart on the drawn line as shown in Figure 2. Repeat to complete four triangle/square units.

Figure 1
Sew 1/4" on each side of the diagonal line.

Figure 2
Cut squares apart on the drawn line.

Step 3. Join four units to complete one block as shown in Figure 3; press. Repeat for 156 blocks.

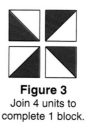

Figure 3
Join 4 units to complete 1 block.

Quilt Top Assembly

Step 1. Arrange the pieced blocks in 13 rows of 12 blocks each referring to the Placement Diagram or photo for placement.

Step 2. Join the blocks in rows; press. Join the rows; press.

Step 3. Cut two strips border fabric 3" x 46"; sew a strip to each side; press seams toward strips. Cut two more strips 3" x 47 1/2"; sew a strip to the top and bottom; press seams toward strips.

Finishing

Step 1. Prepare pieced top for quilting referring to Chapter 5.

Step 2. Quilt in the ditch of the seams of the blocks and as desired on borders by hand or machine.

Step 3. When quilting is complete finish edges referring to Chapter 5.

—By Nancy Paravecchia

Christmas in August
Placement Diagram
47" x 50 1/2"

Victorian Mantel Quilt

If you live in a Victorian-style home, your mantel would be beautiful with this pretty cover. Coordinate your decorations with poinsettia plants around the room to tie your holiday decorations together with a focus on the fireplace.

PROJECT SPECIFICATIONS

Skill Level: Beginner
Project Size: Approximately 18" x 48"

MATERIALS

- 2 yards cotton moiré print
- 2 yards white flannel
- 1 Christmas print pillow panel (1 front, 1 back)
- 1 spool each white and gold all-purpose thread
- 1 spool clear fine monofilament thread
- 1 spool gold metallic thread
- 7 yards gold cord
- 8 gold tassels
- Fusible transfer web
- Basic sewing supplies and tools, chalk pencil or fade-out pen and tracing paper

PROJECT NOTE

The pattern provided is for a standard mantel up to 12" deep and 7' long. Adjust width or length for other sizes.

INSTRUCTIONS

Step 1. Cut a piece of tracing paper 18" x 48". *Note: Tape pieces together as necessary to make paper this size.* Draw a line 10" away from long edge as shown in Figure 1.

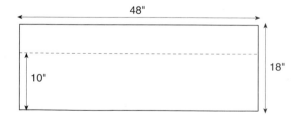

Figure 1
Draw a line 10" away from long edge as shown.

Step 2. Draw a line from top to bottom 12" from one end as shown in Figure 2. Mark 5" up from bottom of this section. Connect this point with previously drawn line as shown in Figure 3. Cut away shaded areas as shown in Figure 4.

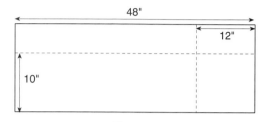

Figure 2
Draw a line from top to bottom 12" from 1 edge.

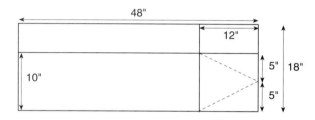

Figure 3
Mark 5" up from bottom; draw lines to connect to previously drawn line to make a triangle as shown.

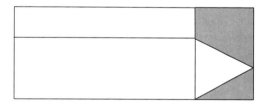

Figure 4
Cut away shaded area as shown.

Step 3. On another piece of tracing paper, draw a triangle as shown in Figure 5. Tape the base of the triangle on tracing paper as shown in Figure 6; trace point with marker. Repeat for three points as shown in Figure 6. Cut away shaded areas.

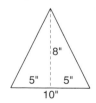

Figure 5
Draw a triangle to make pattern as shown.

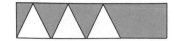

Figure 6
Trace triangles on another piece of paper.

Step 4. Tape the base of the triangle paper on the previously cut pattern as shown in Figure 7. Cut away shaded areas to make half of the mantel quilt pattern.

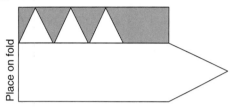

Place on fold

Figure 7
Tape the base of the triangle paper on the previously cut pattern as shown. Cut away shaded areas to make pattern.

Step 5. Cut one on fold of flannel and two on fold of moiré.

Step 6. Place moiré pieces together, right sides facing. Place flannel piece on top; pin and stitch 1/4" away from edge all around, leaving a 4" opening for turning.

Step 7. Trim points and corners; turn. Close opening with white thread; press.

Step 8. Stitch close to edges with gold metallic thread in the top of the machine and white thread in the bobbin.

Step 9. Bond fusible transfer web to wrong side of pillow panels following manufacturer's instructions. Cut motifs from panel using sharp scissors; remove paper backing.

Step 10. Position motifs on points; fuse in place following manufacturer's instructions.

Step 11. Stitch around motifs using a zigzag or blind-hem stitch worked with monofilament thread in the top of the machine and white thread in the bobbin.

Step 12. Mark a 1/2" grid with ruler and chalk pencil (optional). Quilt along grid with gold metallic thread.

Step 13. Stitch cord around outside edges by hand using gold thread. Stitch one tassel to each point to finish.

—By Beth Wheeler

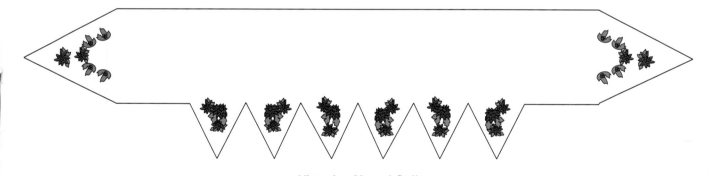

Victorian Mantel Quilt
Placement Diagram
Approximately 18" x 48"

Folk Art Mantel Quilt

This folk art mantel quilt will fit right into your decorating scheme if your home has a country look. It's quick and easy to make. Changing the fabric to scraps of red, white and blue will turn this mantel quilt into a patriotic quilt in celebration of our country.

PROJECT SPECIFICATIONS
Skill Level: Beginner
Project Size: Approximately 18" x 48"

MATERIALS
- 2 yards total print fabrics in the following colors: gold, red, red-and-tan and tan
- 2 yards backing
- 2 yards white flannel
- 1 spool neutral color all-purpose thread
- Black embroidery floss or pearl cotton (for hand stitching) or black buttonhole thread (for machine stitching)
- Fine-point permanent marker
- Fusible transfer web
- Basic sewing supplies and tools, template plastic, chalk pencil or fade-out pen and tracing paper

PROJECT NOTES
A butter tub lid may be substituted for template plastic.

The pattern provided is for a standard mantel up to 12" deep and 7' long. Adjust width or length for other sizes.

INSTRUCTIONS
Step 1. Prewash all fabrics; dry. Press to remove wrinkles.

Step 2. Prepare templates for appliqué shapes using template plastic and patterns given.

Step 3. Refer to Steps 1–4 for *Victorian Mantel Quilt* on page 84.

Step 4. Cut one piece of flannel on fold using pattern.

Step 5. Cut one or two strips each of red, red-and-tan and tan fabrics in the following widths: 1 1/4", 1 1/2", 1 3/4" and 2".

Step 6. Draw a line on the flannel with chalk pencil and ruler as shown in Figure 1. Place first fabric strip along chalk line. Pin a second strip on the first, right sides together. Stitch with a 1/4" seam allowance; finger-press seam open.

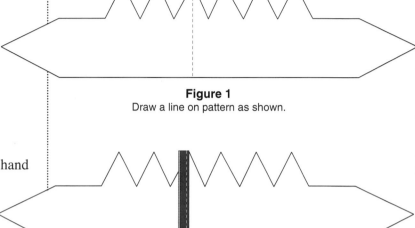

Figure 1
Draw a line on pattern as shown.

Figure 2
Begin sewing first 2 strips onto flannel base as shown.

Step 7. Strip-piece in this manner until entire flannel piece is covered; press. Trim excess to match the shape of the flannel.

Step 8. Place the pieced front on backing fabric, with wrong sides together. Using front as a pattern, cut a backing.

Step 9. Stitch the backing and top together 1/4" away from raw edges all around.

Step 10. Work buttonhole stitches around outside raw edges by hand with 3 strands of embroidery floss or pearl cotton or by machine with buttonhole thread. ***Note:*** *If you prefer a more finished look, place the backing piece right sides together with the pieced top; stitch all around, leaving an opening to turn right side out. Turn right side out; hand-stitch opening closed to finish.*

Step 11. Bond fusible transfer web to wrong side of gold fabrics. Trace 24 stars (a combination of large, medium and small sizes) onto paper side of fabrics; cut out.

Step 12. Remove paper; place stars randomly on points of mantel quilt. Fuse in place according to manufacturer's instructions.

Step 13. Work buttonhole stitches around each star using same method used on edges of mantel quilt to finish.

—By Beth Wheeler

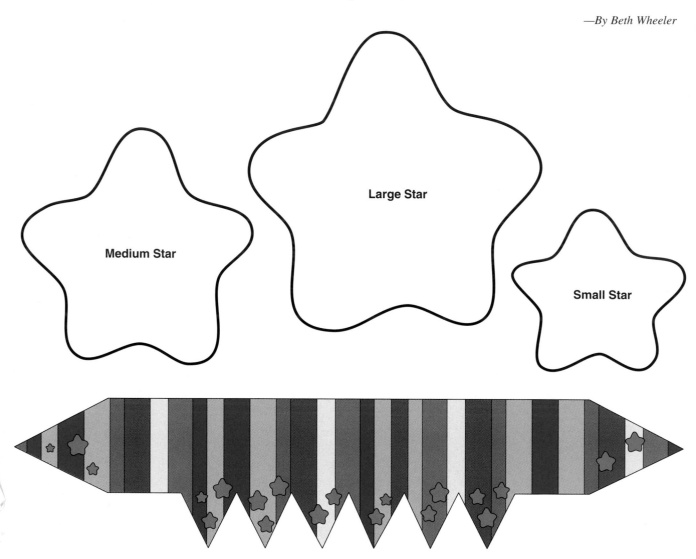

Large Star

Medium Star

Small Star

Folk Art Mantel Quilt
Placement Diagram
Approximately 18" x 48"

Crazy Patchwork Christmas Vest

It's fun to dress up for the holidays. Check out your scrap bag for a variety of colorful Christmas prints to make this easy vest. Piping between the seams adds sparkle.

PROJECT SPECIFICATIONS
Skill Level: Beginner

Vest Size: Any size

MATERIALS
- 1 1/2 yards Christmas print for vest lining and back
- Scraps Christmas prints to total 2/3 yard
- Purchased vest pattern of choice
- 2/3 yard muslin (vest fronts)
- Matching all-purpose thread
- 3 yards gold lamé piping
- Basic sewing supplies and tools and zipper foot

Crazy Patchwork Christmas Vest
Placement Diagram

INSTRUCTIONS
Step 1. Prewash all fabrics; press.

Step 2. Cut out vest fronts from muslin using commercial pattern.

 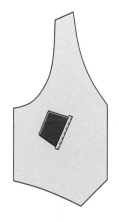

Figure 1
Place a fabric scrap in the center of 1 vest front.

Figure 2
Place piping on scrap.

Step 3. Place one fabric scrap in the center of one vest front as shown in Figure 1. Lay a piece of piping on one edge of the piece as shown in Figure 2. Trim piping a bit longer than the scrap on both ends.

Step 4. Place a second scrap right sides together on top of the first scrap with piping between. With zipper foot on the machine, sew along edge of scrap and close to piping as shown in Figure 3. *Note: Because you can't see the piping, you must use your fingers to feel it through the scrap fabric on top.*

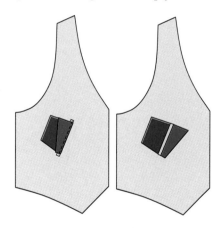

Figure 3
Place second scrap on top of first with piping between; stitch.

Step 5. Repeat this procedure, adding scraps around the first piece. Each new piece will cover the seams of the previous pieces. Refer to the Placement Diagram and photo of project for suggestions.

Step 6. Repeat the crazy-patchwork procedure for the second vest front.

Step 7. Cut vest lining and back; finish vest following instructions given with the commercial pattern.

—By Ann Boyce

Scrap Bag Snail's Trail

It won't take you long to stitch this creative wall quilt! Sort through your scraps, choosing all the traditional Christmas colors, then follow the snail's trail to make an eye-catching holiday project.

PROJECT SPECIFICATIONS
Skill Level: Intermediate
Quilt Size: 23" x 23"

MATERIALS

- Scraps of 6–8 different green, 6–9 different red and 8–10 different cream print or solid fabrics
- 1/2 yard dark green print
- 1/4 yard red print
- Backing 26" x 26"
- Batting 26" x 26"
- Matching all-purpose thread
- 1 spool contrasting quilting thread
- Basic sewing tools and supplies, rotary cutter, mat and ruler

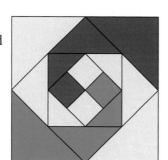

Snail's Trail
3" x 3" Block

PROJECT NOTE
Before beginning, photocopy the paper foundation pattern 12 times, checking that copy is the same size as the original. Trim excess paper from copies, leaving a narrow margin beyond outer cutting line.

Cutting
Note: A 1/4" seam allowance is included in all measurements.

Step 1. Cut two strips dark green print 1 1/4" x 15 1/2" (A) and two strips 1 1/4" x 17" (B). Cut 1 1/2"-wide bias strips from dark green print to total 94" when seamed together.

Step 2. Cut two strips red print 3 1/2" x 17" (C) and two strips 3 1/2" x 23" (D).

Step 3. For foundation blocks, cut the following using a different fabric for each green, red and cream fabric listed: one each green and red and two cream strips 1 1/4" x 15" for center Four-Patch units; six each green and red and six each of two different cream fabric squares 1 3/4" x 1 3/4" for

triangles 5–8; six each green and red and six each of two different cream fabric squares 2 1/4" x 2 1/4" for triangles 9–12; and six each green and red and six each of two different cream fabric squares 2 3/4" x 2 3/4" for triangles 13–16.

Step 4. Cut each square in half diagonally to make triangles.

Step 5. Cut four different cream, four different green and five different red squares 3 1/2" x 3 1/2" for alternate plain blocks.

Paper Piecing
Step 1. Sew the 1 1/4" x 17" strips as follows: cream to green and cream to red; press seams toward darker fabric. Cut each strip section into twelve 1 1/4" sections as shown in Figure 1.
Step 2. Join pairs of red and green sections into 12

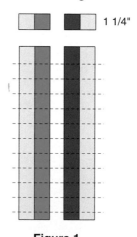

1 1/4"

Figure 1
Cut each stitched strip
into 1 1/4" sections.

Four-Patch units, rotating so opposite colors align. Position each Four-Patch against the blank side of a paper foundation; align center of cross lines with patchwork cross seams, also matching fabric colors to foundation; pin or baste in place. *Note: To assist with alignment, insert a pin through paper at center intersections; insert at same spot on fabric patch. Hold toward light to see through to check accuracy.*

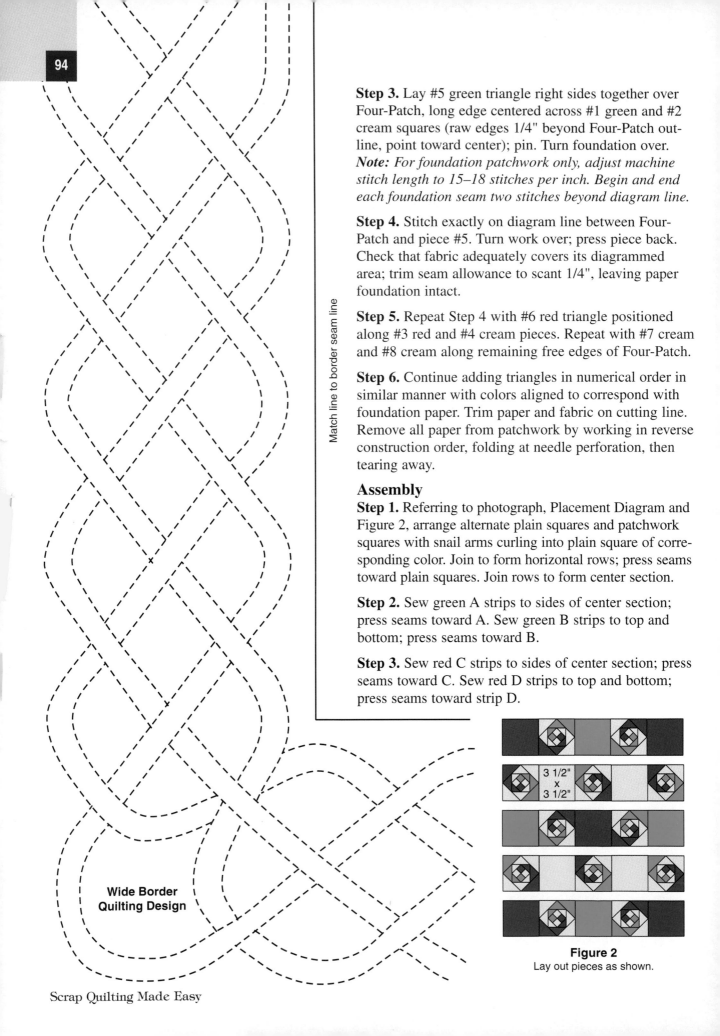

Wide Border Quilting Design

Match line to border seam line

Step 3. Lay #5 green triangle right sides together over Four-Patch, long edge centered across #1 green and #2 cream squares (raw edges 1/4" beyond Four-Patch outline, point toward center); pin. Turn foundation over. *Note: For foundation patchwork only, adjust machine stitch length to 15–18 stitches per inch. Begin and end each foundation seam two stitches beyond diagram line.*

Step 4. Stitch exactly on diagram line between Four-Patch and piece #5. Turn work over; press piece back. Check that fabric adequately covers its diagrammed area; trim seam allowance to scant 1/4", leaving paper foundation intact.

Step 5. Repeat Step 4 with #6 red triangle positioned along #3 red and #4 cream pieces. Repeat with #7 cream and #8 cream along remaining free edges of Four-Patch.

Step 6. Continue adding triangles in numerical order in similar manner with colors aligned to correspond with foundation paper. Trim paper and fabric on cutting line. Remove all paper from patchwork by working in reverse construction order, folding at needle perforation, then tearing away.

Assembly

Step 1. Referring to photograph, Placement Diagram and Figure 2, arrange alternate plain squares and patchwork squares with snail arms curling into plain square of corresponding color. Join to form horizontal rows; press seams toward plain squares. Join rows to form center section.

Step 2. Sew green A strips to sides of center section; press seams toward A. Sew green B strips to top and bottom; press seams toward B.

Step 3. Sew red C strips to sides of center section; press seams toward C. Sew red D strips to top and bottom; press seams toward strip D.

Figure 2
Lay out pieces as shown.

Finishing

Step 1. Transfer Wide Border Quilting Design to fabric, matching solid line to border seam line. Begin at corners and work toward the center. Complete all four corners with pattern as shown, then flip pattern, align and complete adjacent sides, connecting straight lines at border centers.

Step 2. Mark square-in-a-square quilting lines in plain squares by connecting or extending largest triangle seams as shown in Figure 3.

Figure 3
Mark square-in-a-square quilting
design in plain squares as shown.

Step 3. Sandwich the batting between the marked quilt top and the prepared backing piece. Baste layers together to hold flat. Quilt on marked lines and in the ditch around red and green snail arms and at inside edges of narrow and wide border strips.

Step 4. When quilting is complete, trim edges even and remove basting.

Step 5. Prepare self-made binding and finish edges of quilt referring to Chapter 5 for instructions.

—*By Jodi Warner*

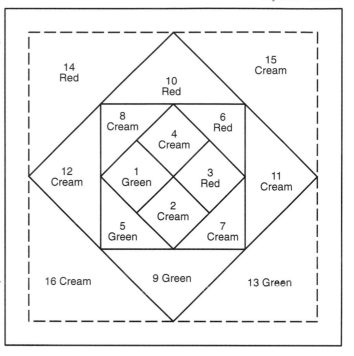

Full-Size Paper-Piecing Foundation
Make 12 copies

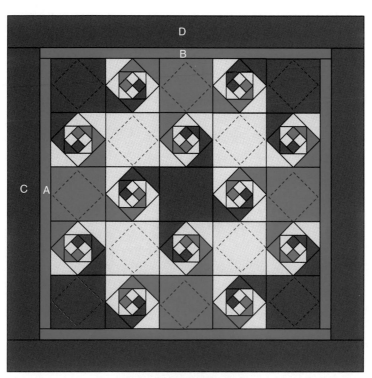

Scrap Bag Snail's Trail
Placement Diagram
23" x 23"
(includes binding)

Treeflake

As the trees turn to gold, red and orange, and the snow begins to fall, gather together your scraps in the same colors to make this pretty pieced wall quilt.

PROJECT SPECIFICATIONS
Skill Level: Intermediate
Quilt Size: 47" x 47"

MATERIALS
- 1 fat quarter each of 8 different prints or scraps to total 1 yard for trees
- 1/2 yard brown print for tree trunks
- 3 yards white-on-white print
- 1/4 yard green print for inner border
- 1 1/2 yards print for outside border and binding
- Neutral color all-purpose thread
- Basic sewing tools and supplies

Treeflake
16" x 16" Block

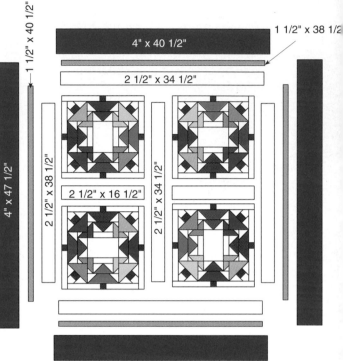

Figure 2
Arrange blocks and border strips as shown.

INSTRUCTIONS
Step 1. Cut two strips white-on-white print 2 1/2" x 34 1/2" and two strips 2 1/2" x 38 1/2" for inside border frame.

Step 2. Cut two strips green print 1 1/2" x 38 1/2" and two strips 1 1/2" x 40 1/2" for inner border.

Step 3. Cut two strips print 4" x 40 1/2" and two strips 4" x 47 1/2" for outer border.

Step 4. Cut two white-on-white sashing strips 2 1/2" x 16 1/2" and one strip 2 1/2" x 34 1/2".

Step 5. Prepare 5 1/4 yards self-made binding from print referring to Chapter 5.

Step 6. Piece one Tree Block referring to Figure 1; repeat for four blocks.

Step 7. Arrange the completed blocks in two rows of two blocks referring to Figure 2 for placement. *Note: Each block is turned to give trees a different placement.* Sew blocks together in rows; join rows; press seams. Join the rows; press.

Step 8. Sew framing and border strips to sides and top and bottom in the order shown in Figure 2; press seams toward border strips.

Step 9. Mark the quilting designs given onto completed top using water-erasable marker or pencil. Refer to photo.

Step 10. Sandwich batting between the completed top and prepared backing piece. Baste or pin layers together to hold flat for quilting.

Step 11. Quilt on marked lines and in the ditch of tree shapes by hand or machine. When quilting is complete, trim edges even.

Step 12. Bind edges using self-made binding referring to Chapter 5.

—By Lisa Christensen

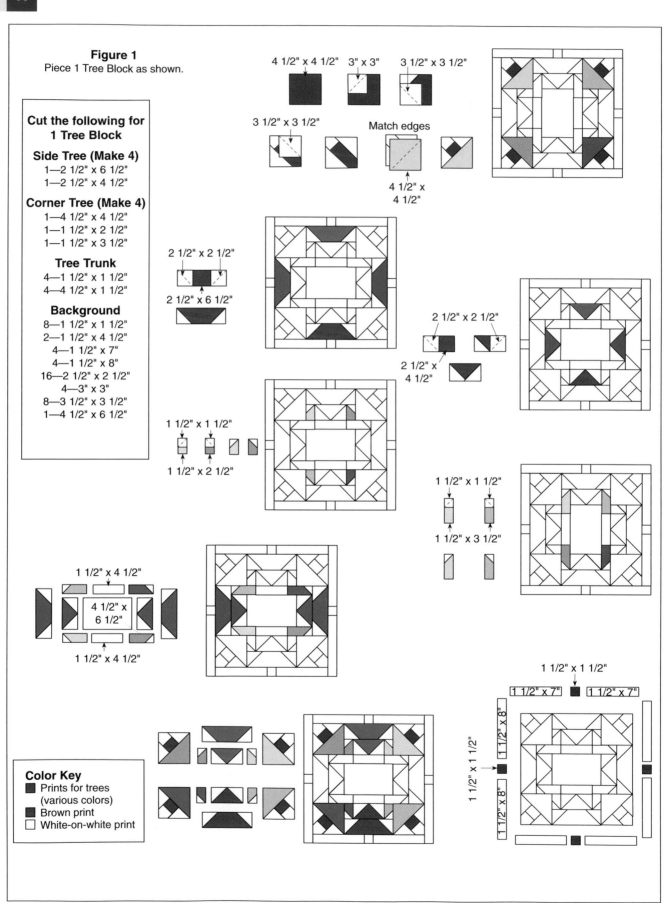

Figure 1
Piece 1 Tree Block as shown.

4 1/2" x 4 1/2"   3" x 3"   3 1/2" x 3 1/2"

3 1/2" x 3 1/2"   Match edges

4 1/2" x 4 1/2"

Cut the following for 1 Tree Block

Side Tree (Make 4)
1—2 1/2" x 6 1/2"
1—2 1/2" x 4 1/2"

Corner Tree (Make 4)
1—4 1/2" x 4 1/2"
1—1 1/2" x 2 1/2"
1—1 1/2" x 3 1/2"

Tree Trunk
4—1 1/2" x 1 1/2"
4—4 1/2" x 1 1/2"

Background
8—1 1/2" x 1 1/2"
2—1 1/2" x 4 1/2"
4—1 1/2" x 7"
4—1 1/2" x 8"
16—2 1/2" x 2 1/2"
4—3" x 3"
8—3 1/2" x 3 1/2"
1—4 1/2" x 6 1/2"

2 1/2" x 2 1/2"

2 1/2" x 6 1/2"

2 1/2" x 2 1/2"

2 1/2" x 4 1/2"

1 1/2" x 1 1/2"

1 1/2" x 2 1/2"

1 1/2" x 1 1/2"

1 1/2" x 3 1/2"

1 1/2" x 4 1/2"

4 1/2" x 6 1/2"

1 1/2" x 4 1/2"

1 1/2" x 1 1/2"

1 1/2" x 7"   1 1/2" x 7"

1 1/2" x 8"

1 1/2" x 1 1/2"

1 1/2" x 8"

Color Key
▪ Prints for trees (various colors)
▪ Brown print
☐ White-on-white print

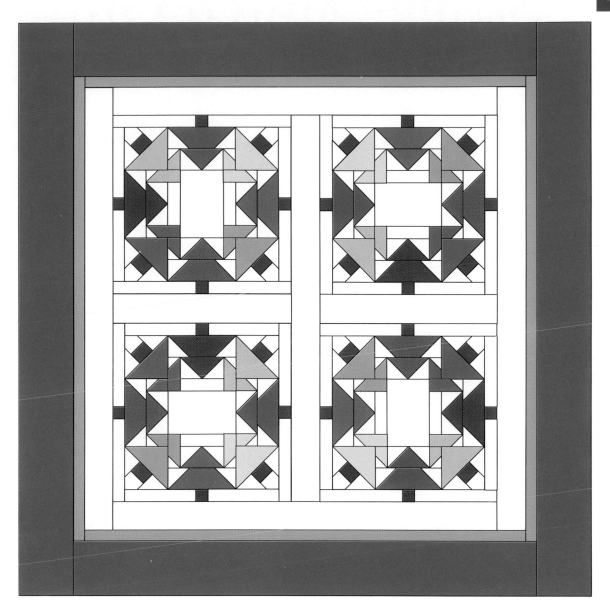

Treeflake
Placement Diagram
47" x 47"

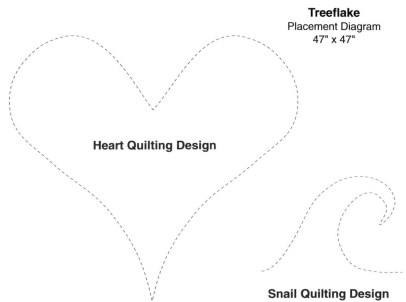

Heart Quilting Design

Snail Quilting Design

Scrap Quilting Made Easy

String-Quilted Gift Bags & String of Stars

Everyone knows you are a quilter. Don't they secretly expect a quilted gift for every holiday? Make it easy on yourself and give a gift in one of these neat string-quilted gift bags. For your home, hang a string of stuffed stars in a doorway, on a tree or mantel or along a staircase to add a patch of color and some spirit to your holiday decor.

String-Quilted Gift Bags

PROJECT SPECIFICATIONS
Skill Level: Beginner

Bag Sizes: Approximately 4" x 6", 6" x 8 1/2" and 9" x 11"

MATERIALS
- Assorted Christmas print strips in various widths
- 2 pieces each fabric stabilizer 8 1/2" x 7 1/2", 9 1/2" x 11" and 12 1/2" x 13 1/2"
- 1/2 yard ribbon or cord for handles
- Rayon or metallic thread
- 1 spool contrasting quilting thread
- Basic sewing supplies, template plastic, rotary cutter, mat and ruler

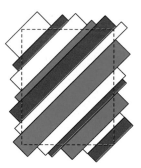

String-Quilted Gift Bags
Placement Diagram

Assembly
Step 1. Use two same-size fabric stabilizer pieces. Starting in one corner of one piece, add strips right sides together as shown in Figure 1. Flip stitched strip; press. Continue adding strips until foundation

is covered, varying the width of the strips from 3/4" to 3". Repeat for second foundation.

Step 2. Stitch around the patchwork close to outside edges. Trim edges square with foundation piece as shown in Figure 2; do not remove the stabilizer.

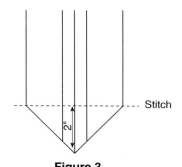

Figure 2
Trim edges square with foundation.

Step 3. Add machine embroidery using rayon or metallic thread at this time if desired.

Finishing
Step 1. Sew two string-pieced foundation pieces with right sides together around three sides using a 1/4" seam allowance. Measure and mark 2" from the corner on seam line on both sides. Draw a line

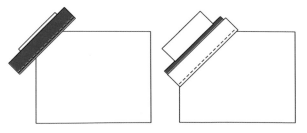

Figure 1
Flip stitched piece up; press flat.

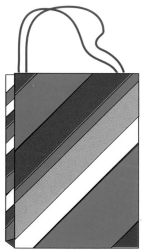

Stitch

Figure 3
Measure and mark 2" from corner. Stitch across to make square bottom.

Weekend Project

MAKE IN 24 HOURS OR LESS • MAKE IN 24 HOURS OR LESS • MAKE IN 24 HOURS OR LESS •
OR LESS • MAKE IN 24 HOURS OR LESS • MAKE IN

at this point perpendicular to seam line; stitch on this line referring to Figure 3. *Note: It should be a small triangle on the corner.* Repeat for other side of bag.

Step 2. Turn right side out. Lay bag on its side; press creases with steam iron 1 1/2" from both side seams from top to bottom as shown in Figure 4.

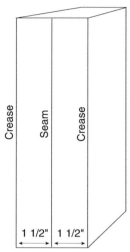

Figure 4
Press creases 1 1/2" from each side
seam from top to bottom.

Step 3. Turn top edge 3/4" to inside; press. Open out again and clean-finish (serge or turn under and hem) top edge. Cut cord in half; position on inside of bag front and back 7/8" (1 1/2") (2") in from creases on both sides. Stitch in place with raw edges of cord even with top edge of bag. Turn hemmed edge back to inside; topstitch in place to finish.

String of Stars

PROJECT SPECIFICATIONS
Skill Level: Beginner
String Size: 6" x 23"

MATERIALS
Pinwheel Stars

- 2 strips each 1" by fabric width red, white and green Christmas prints

Scrap Stars

- 24 assorted 3" squares various Christmas prints
- 1 spool metallic machine embroidery thread

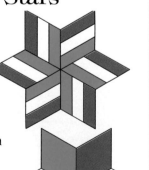

Each Project

- 1 1/3 yards 3/8"-wide ribbon
- 4 gold bells
- 1 spool matching all-purpose thread
- Backing fabric 8" by fabric width or 4 scrap 8" squares
- Fiberfill stuffing
- Basic sewing supplies, template plastic, rotary cutter, mat and ruler with 60-degree line

Pinwheel Star Assembly
Step 1. Sew one red, white and green strip together along long edges; press seams in one direction. Repeat with other three strips.

Step 2. With ruler, cut left side of strip off at a 60-degree angle. Move ruler over 2" and make another cut. Referring to Figure 1, continue cutting in this manner to end of strip; repeat for second strip. *Note: A template has been provided for use if a ruler with a 60-degree angle is not available.*

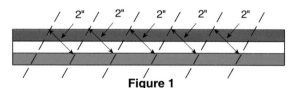

Figure 1
Cut strip at 60-degree angle every 2".

Step 3. Arrange diamonds in groups of three; sew together referring to Figure 2. Press seams all in the same direction. Sew two groups of three together across center. Repeat for four *Pinwheel Stars*, two of each variation.

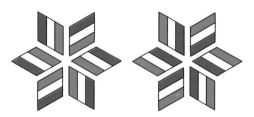

Figure 2
Join diamonds to make Pinwheel Stars.

Step 4. Machine-embroider across center seams of stars using metallic thread and a fancy stitch, if desired.

Step 5. Lay pieced star right side down on a square of backing fabric. Using the pieced star as a pattern, cut backing to fit.

Step 6. Place backing and pieced star unit right sides together. Sew around outside edges, leaving opening to turn; turn right side out through opening. Repeat for all stars.

Step 7. Stuff with fiberfill. Slipstitch opening closed.

Step 8. Sew a bell to the center of each star. Join stars together with a few hand stitches at points to make a string.

Step 9. Cut ribbon in half. Fold each piece in half and stitch one piece to each end for hanging.

Scrap Star Assembly

Step 1. Using the template provided, cut 24 diamonds from assorted prints.

Step 2. Complete star shapes referring to Steps 3–9 for *Pinwheel Star* and Figure 3.

—*By Karen Neary*

Star Template
Cut 24 scraps

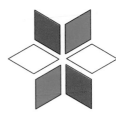

Figure 3
Join diamonds to
make Scrap Stars.

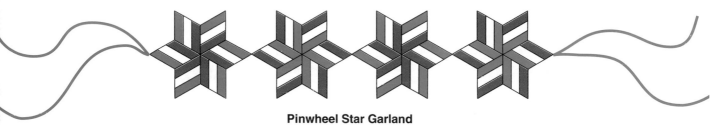

Pinwheel Star Garland
Placement Diagram
6" x 24"

Scrap Star Garland
Placement Diagram
6" x 24"

Scrap Quilting Made Easy

Special-Occasion Quilts

Squashed Double Wedding Ring

This longtime favorite design is perfect for emptying your scrap basket, a wonderful change of pace from quick-to-make projects. You'll enjoy working with your fabric scraps as you plan and stitch this heirloom-quality quilt.

PROJECT SPECIFICATIONS
Skill Level: Experienced

Quilt Size: Approximately 76 1/2" x 86 3/4"

MATERIALS
- 4 1/2 yards assorted print and solid scraps
- 3 yards unbleached muslin
- 3 yards pink solid with mini-figure
- 1/2 yard goldenrod solid-look print
- Backing 81" x 91"
- Batting 81" x 91"
- Neutral color all-purpose thread
- Basic sewing tools and supplies, template plastic and tracing paper

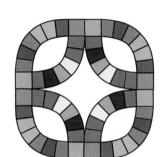

Squashed Wedding Ring
10 1/4" x 10 1/4" Block

PROJECT NOTES
Transfer finished-size templates for all pieces onto template plastic.

Traditional hand-piecing is the construction technique recommended because of the accuracy it allows. For this reason templates are shown without seam allowances included. Template shapes should be traced onto the wrong side of fabrics, then cut out with an accurate 1/4" seam allowance added. To assist with alignment of pieces, transfer hashmarks to templates; transfer marks with pencil to fabric patches as they are being traced.

To make one long border strip for each color, trace template onto tracing paper to make one long pattern; or trace pattern as directed onto border fabric, tracing the pattern five times for top and bottom and six times for side border strips. Trace corner pieces at each end, reversing piece for one end.

If you prefer, make the large borders as one piece and appliqué a binding strip for the trim piece. Use trim line on pattern pieces as a guide for placement.

Cutting
Step 1. Prepare templates for each pattern piece. Cut eight of each A–D and BR–DR from scraps, four muslin E's and one muslin F for each block.

Step 2. Cut the following from pink: two long K and G inside border sections with six K and G units, adding H and L to one end and HR and LR to the other end (making one long piece). Repeat for two strips with five K and G units. Cut two goldenrod strips using six I Trim Border units and one each J and J reversed units for sides and two strips using five I Trim Border units with J and J reversed for top and bottom. *Note: Use templates laid side by side to trace long border sections as directed, first tracing a guideline on fabric to ensure straight-of-grain alignment.*

Step 3. Sew the K, G, H and L pieces together with J and I pieces between to make border strips; set aside.

Piecing
Step 1. To piece one block sew B to C to D to DR to CR to BR to form eight arch sections, pressing seams toward B end. Join inner edge of one arch section to one side of E, aligning center notch marks with D-DR seams as shown in Figure 1; press seam toward arch. Repeat for four units.

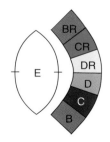

Figure 1
Sew B to C to D to DR
to CR to BR; join to E.

Figure 2
Sew A squares to the end
of remaining arch units.

Step 2. Sew A squares to ends of remaining four arch sections as shown in Figure 2; press seam toward A. Join each section to remaining curved edge of E arch units; press seams toward arch.

Step 3. Clip curved edges of seam allowance on F piece at regular 1/4" intervals, stopping short of traced seam line. Join one double-arch unit to F, matching center marks with D-DR seam and positioning point at B or BR marks; press seam toward arch. Join remaining three double-arch units in similar manner as shown in Figure 3. Repeat for 42 blocks.

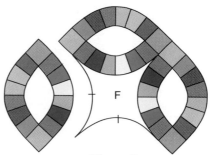

Figure 3
Sew pieced units to F to
complete 1 block.

Squashed Double Wedding Ring
Placement Diagram
Approximately 76 1/2" x 86 3/4"

Step 4. Join six blocks side by side by aligning the flat center side sections at A patches between B and BR marks of adjacent rings as shown in Figure 4; complete seven rows.

Figure 4
Join blocks in rows, matching marks on pieces.

Figure 6
Trace Inner border piece 5 times for short borders; trace an Outer border piece on each end, reversing on 1 end. Stay-stitch H and G as shown.

Figure 5
Set in piece F as shown.

Step 5. At the inside edge of the first row, clip and insert five F pieces into the spaces between rings as shown in Figure 5; stitch; press seam toward rings. Insert free edges of F into appropriate spaces between rings of next row, align marks and seams; stitch to join. Press seams toward rings. Continue inserting and joining until all rows are complete.

Step 6. Reinforce inside each corner and all traced border sections by completing a short stay-stitch (with closely matched thread) by hand exactly on traced seam line and 1/2" on each side of angle point as shown in Figure 6. Carefully clip at each inside corner, stopping just short of stay-stitching. Clip inside curves at regular 1/4" intervals. Align, join Inner, Trim and Outer border lengths to prepare two long and two short border units; press seams toward outer edge.

Step 7. Insert points of border sections into spaces between rings along matching edges of center panel; stitch, matching marks at A/A and B-BR seams; press seam under rings. As adjacent borders are attached, miter corner seams; press completed top.

Half-Feathered Fan Quilting Design
Align and trace; flip to trace opposite half

Align with outer Trim seam

Align centered between Ring spaces

Finishing

Step 1. Mark double diagonal lines 1/4" apart through E and F centers to form a grid design referring to marks on templates.

Step 2. Mark a single quilting line around the center of each ring. Transfer Feather Fan and Feather Arch patterns onto borders.

Step 3. Sandwich the batting between the marked quilt top and the prepared backing piece. Baste layers together to hold flat. Quilt on marked lines and in the ditch close to all patchwork seams and 1/8" away from patchwork on inside borders.

Step 4. When quilting is complete, trim edges even and remove basting.

Step 5. Prepare 8 1/2 yards double-fold bias binding using pink fabric referring to Chapter 5 to finish.

—By Jodi Warner

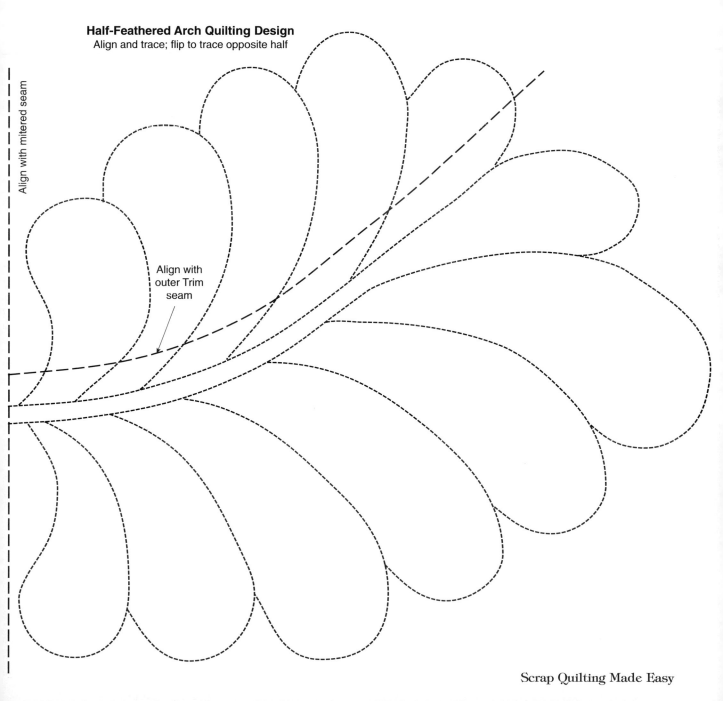

Half-Feathered Arch Quilting Design
Align and trace; flip to trace opposite half

Align with mitered seam

Align with outer Trim seam

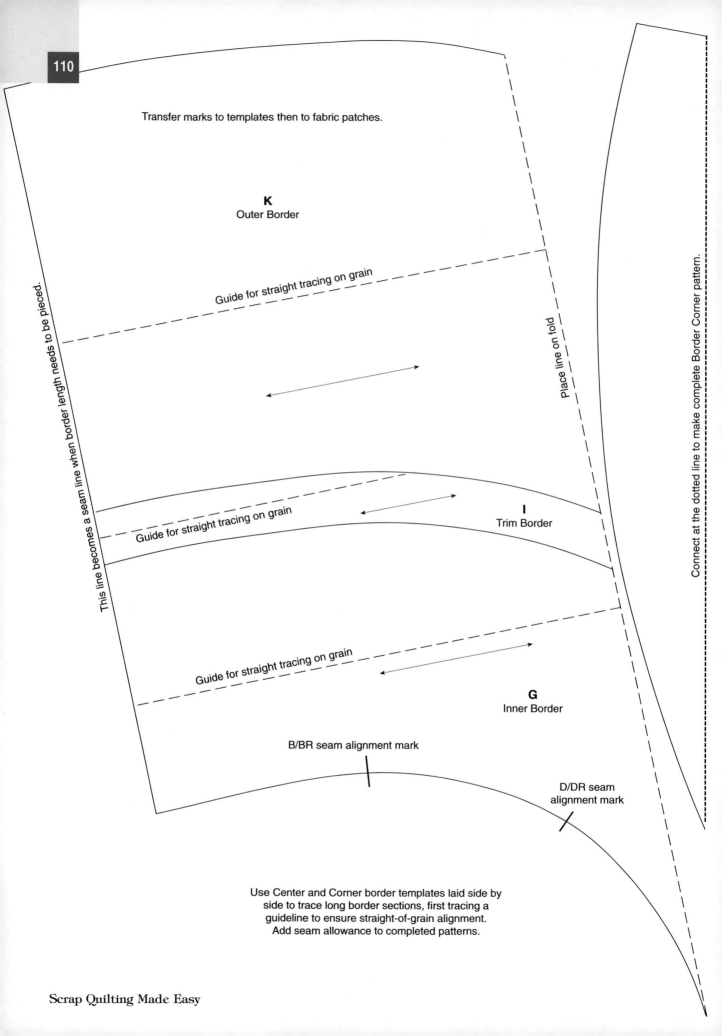

Transfer marks to templates then to fabric patches.

K
Outer Border

Guide for straight tracing on grain

Place line on fold

Connect at the dotted line to make complete Border Corner pattern.

This line becomes a seam line when border length needs to be pieced.

Guide for straight tracing on grain

I
Trim Border

Guide for straight tracing on grain

G
Inner Border

B/BR seam alignment mark

D/DR seam
alignment mark

Use Center and Corner border templates laid side by
side to trace long border sections, first tracing a
guideline to ensure straight-of-grain alignment.
Add seam allowance to completed patterns.

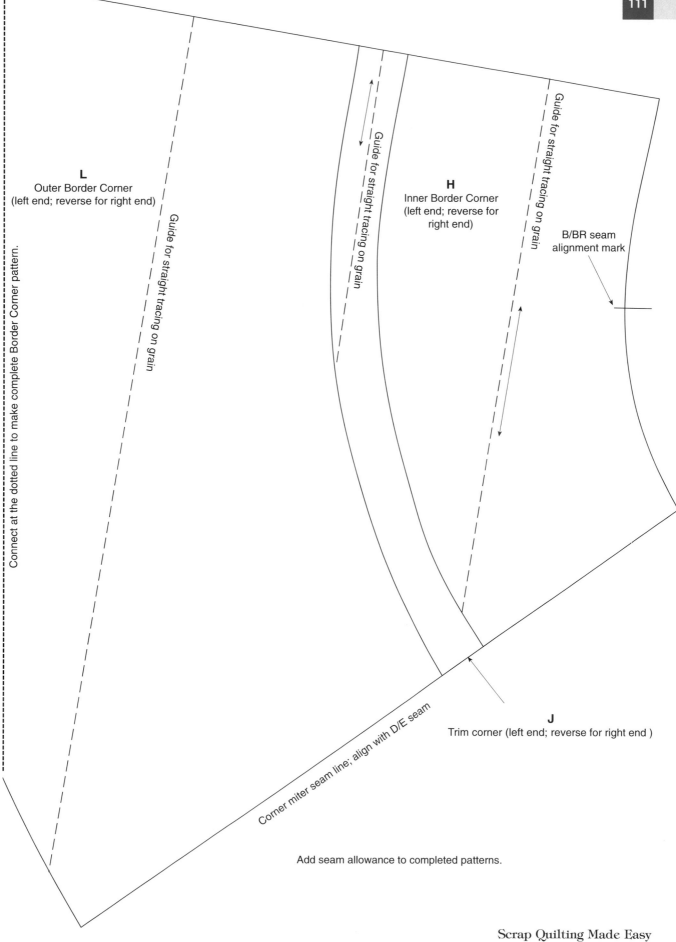

L
Outer Border Corner
(left end; reverse for right end)

Connect at the dotted line to make complete Border Corner pattern.

Guide for straight tracing on grain

Guide for straight tracing on grain

Guide for straight tracing on grain

H
Inner Border Corner
(left end; reverse for right end)

B/BR seam alignment mark

Corner miter seam line; align with D/E seam

J
Trim corner (left end; reverse for right end)

Add seam allowance to completed patterns.

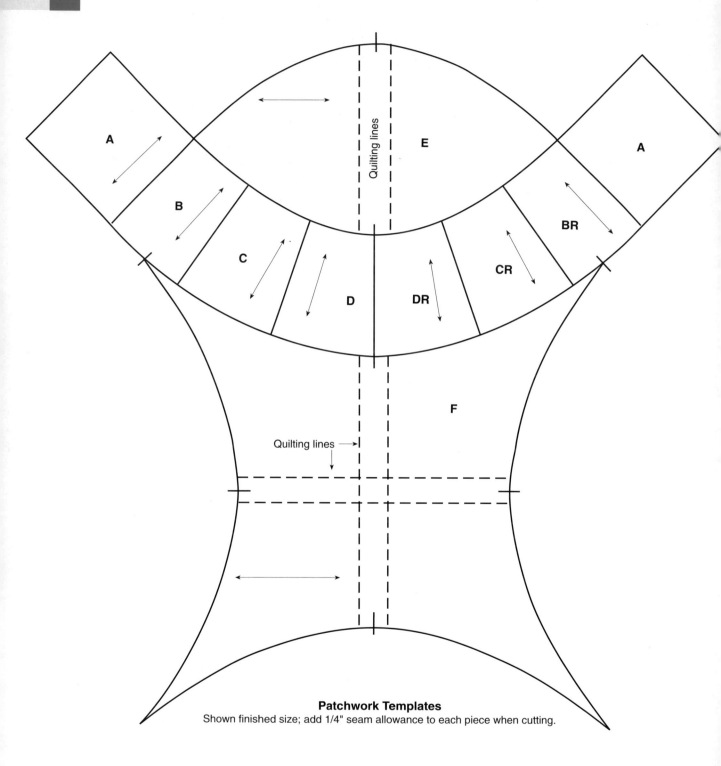

A

E

Quilting lines

A

B

BR

C

CR

D

DR

F

Quilting lines →

Patchwork Templates
Shown finished size; add 1/4" seam allowance to each piece when cutting.

Folk Art Sweatshirt Jacket

What could be more fun than a sweatshirt with patches made from your favorite quilt scraps? You'll love the fit of our folk-art jacket made from a simple sweatshirt. The edges are finished with buttonhole stitches, and old buttons complete the perfect look for yourself or to give as a gift to your favorite quilter.

PROJECT SPECIFICATIONS
Skill Level: Beginner

Size: Any size

MATERIALS
- Off-white sweatshirt with set-in sleeves at least 1 size larger than you normally wear
- Scraps plaid fabric
- 1 square fabric 21" x 21"
- Fusible transfer web
- 1 spool brown pearl cotton or carpet thread
- 1 spool neutral color all-purpose thread
- 4 flat and assorted smaller buttons
- Assorted charms or quilting buttons
- Seam sealant
- Basic sewing tools and supplies, tracing paper, embroidery needle and fade-out pen

INSTRUCTIONS
Step 1. Wash and dry sweatshirt, using no fabric softener.

Step 2. Cut the 21" blue-plaid square in half diagonally for continuous bias binding as shown in Figure 1.

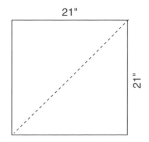

Figure 1
Cut 21" square on the diagonal.

Step 3. With right sides together, stitch the two triangles together as shown in Figure 2. Mark lines

every 2 1/4" on the wrong side of fabric with ruler and pencil or fade-out pen as shown in Figure 3.

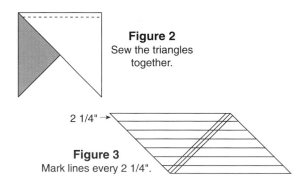

Figure 2
Sew the triangles together.

Figure 3
Mark lines every 2 1/4".

Step 4. Bring the short ends together, right sides facing, offsetting drawn lines by one line. Stitch to make a tube as shown in Figure 4. ***Note:*** *The piece will feel awkward.*

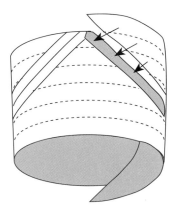

Figure 4
Sew short ends together,
offsetting lines to make a tube.

Step 5. Begin cutting at point A; follow cutting lines in a spiral fashion until all bias is cut in one continuous strip as shown in Figure 5.

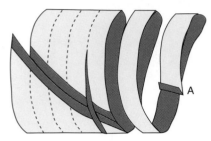

Figure 5
Cut along marked lines, starting at A.

Step 6. Fold binding in half lengthwise, wrong sides together, to make one long folded strip; press.

Step 7. Mark center front line on sweatshirt with fade-out pen. Cut along center front; cut off waistband, cuffs and neck band.

Step 8. Stitch bias binding along outside of shirt and sleeves using a 3/8" seam allowance with raw edges even. Fold binding to inside of sweatshirt; stitch in place by hand.

Step 9. Cut four buttonholes to accommodate flat buttons. Work buttonhole stitches around each hole.

Embellishing
Step 1. Draw a loose, wavy line around neck, front edges and hem using fade-out pen. Work a running stitch along the line with brown thread pearl cotton or carpet thread using an embroidery needle.

Step 2. Place tracing paper over the heart pattern. Trace and cut out; or, cut your own patch shapes from paper.

Step 3. Bond the fusible transfer web to the wrong side of fabric scraps, following manufacturer's instructions. Trace several hearts, a few squares or your chosen shapes on the paper side; cut out. Remove paper backing.

Step 4. Arrange the shapes along the stitched wavy line, overlapping some shapes. Fuse in place following manufacturer's instructions.

Step 5. Work straight stitches around each patch using brown pearl cotton or carpet thread and an embroidery needle.

Step 6. Hand-stitch buttons and charms randomly over sweatshirt front using neutral color thread. Apply a dot of seam sealant on each knot to secure buttons.

—By Beth Wheeler

Folk Art Sweatshirt Jacket
Placement Diagram

Heart
Cut desired number from scraps

Scrappy Heart Jacket

Take a soft and comfortable sweatshirt and add some red and/or pink fabric scrap hearts to dress it up a bit. This quick and easy project makes a wonderful gift for all ages of mothers and daughters.

PROJECT SPECIFICATIONS

Skill Level:
  Beginner
Size: Any size

MATERIALS

- 1 purchased sweatshirt
- Scraps of pink prints to total 1/2 yard
- 1 1/3 yards heavy-duty fusible transfer web
- 1 yard tear-off fabric stabilizer
- 4 spools pink all-purpose thread
- Basic sewing supplies and zigzag sewing machine

INSTRUCTIONS

Step 1. Prepare heart template using pattern given.

Step 2. Press fusible webbing onto pink scraps following manufacturer's instructions. Trace and cut hearts from scraps. *Note: The project shown uses 30 hearts.*

Step 3. Remove ribbing from sweatshirt neck and bottom edges.

Step 4. Pin hearts around neck edge, around bottom edge and two rows down center of sweatshirt, turning hearts as shown in Figure 1.

Scrappy Heart Jacket
Placement Diagram
Any Size

Figure 1
Arrange hearts around neck and bottom and down center of sweatshirt, turning hearts as shown.

Step 5. Remove paper backing from each heart; fuse in place following manufacturer's instructions.

Step 6. Pin tear-off stabilizer behind hearts; zigzag around the outside edge of each heart in a continuous line as shown in Figure 2.

Step 7. Repeat stitching around inside edges in a continuous line as shown in Figure 3.

Figure 2
Sew a continuous line around hearts as shown.

Figure 3
Finish sewing around hearts in 1 continuous line.

Step 8. Pull off stabilizer; trim close to stitching around outside edges of hearts through sweatshirt material. On center front, cut between heart rows to make a cardigan.

—By Ann Boyce

Heart
Cut 30 pink scraps

Bit o' Luck

Decorating for St. Patrick's Day usually involves green shamrocks. As a quilter you can do much better than the cardboard ones you can buy at any gift shop. Make this wall quilt using your scraps of green fabrics and surprise family and friends with your creativity.

PROJECT SPECIFICATIONS
Skill Level: Intermediate
Quilt Size: 25" x 25"
Block Size: 5" x 5", 3" x 5" and 2" x 5"
Number of Blocks: 13

MATERIALS
- 1 fat quarter each of the following: light and dark green prints for shamrocks, brown print for pipes and red plaid for bow blocks and borders
- 1 yard white-on-white print
- Scraps dark green for bow block centers and gray print for pipe smoke
- 1/2 yard dark green print for borders and binding
- All-purpose threads to match fabrics
- 1 spool clear nylon monofilament thread
- Backing 28" x 28"
- Batting 28" x 28"

Shamrock Block
5" x 5" Block

Pipe Block
3" x 5" Block

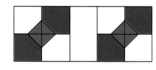

Bow Tie Block
2" x 5" Block

Piecing the Blocks
Step 1. Cut pieces as directed in each chart in Figures 1, 2 and 3 for blocks referring to the Color Keys, the photo and Placement Diagram for color suggestions.

Step 2. To piece one Shamrock block, place a 1" x 1" white-on-white background square on a light green print 1 1/2" x 2" rectangle. Sew across the diagonal as shown in Figure 1; repeat on other end. Press back the stitched triangle; trim excess layers if desired. Repeat for two units.

Step 3. Continue sewing pieces referring to Figure 1 for sizes and colors to join using the same method

used in Step 2. When all units are complete, join in rows; join the rows to complete one block; repeat for five Shamrock blocks.

Step 4. To make one Bow Tie block, layer and stitch pieces referring to Figure 2 to piece units. Arrange the pieced units to complete one block; repeat for four Bow Tie blocks.

Step 5. To make one Pipe block, layer and stitch pieces referring to Figure 3 to piece units. Arrange the pieced units to complete one block; repeat for four Pipe blocks.

Assembly
Step 1. Arrange the pieced blocks in rows referring to the Placement Diagram. Join in rows; join rows to complete center. Press.

Step 2. Cut two strips white-on-white 2" x 15 1/2" and two strips 2" x 18 1/2". Sew short strips to sides and long strips to top and bottom; press seams toward strips.

Step 3. Cut two strips red plaid 1 1/2" x 18 1/2" and two strips 1 1/2" x 20 1/2". Sew short strips to sides and long strips to top and bottom; press seams toward strips.

Step 4. Cut two strips dark green print 3" x 20 1/2" and two strips 3" x 25 1/2". Sew short strips to sides and long strips to top and bottom; press seams toward strips.

Finishing
Step 1. Prepare quilt top for quilting referring to instructions in Chapter 5.

Step 2. Quilt in the ditch of seams and as desired by machine using clear nylon monofilament thread in the top of the machine and all-purpose thread to match backing fabric in the bobbin.

Step 3. Prepare binding from dark green print and finish edges referring to Chapter 5 for instructions.

—By Lisa Christensen

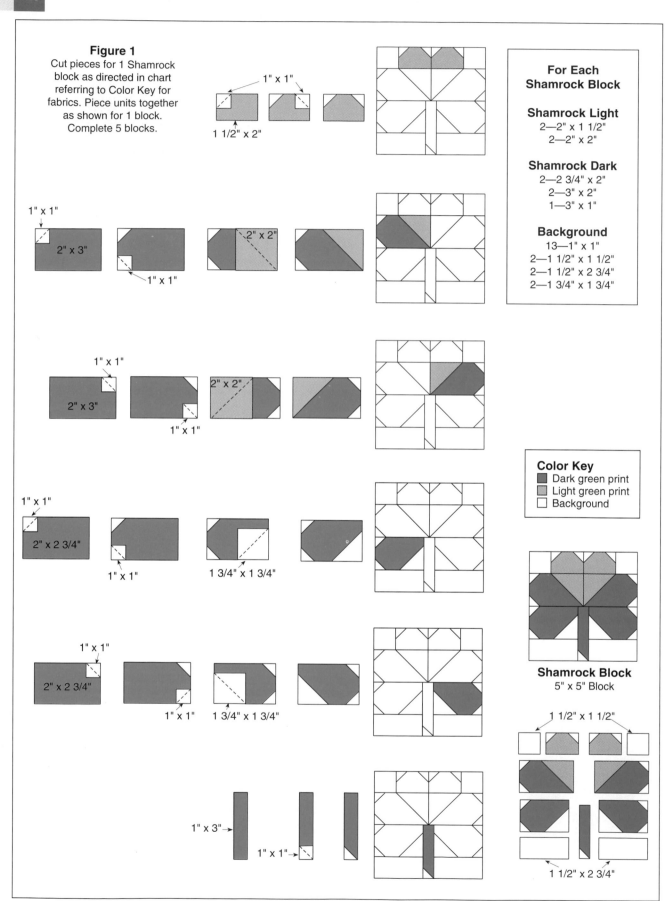

Figure 1
Cut pieces for 1 Shamrock block as directed in chart referring to Color Key for fabrics. Piece units together as shown for 1 block. Complete 5 blocks.

1" x 1"

1 1/2" x 2"

1" x 1"

2" x 3"

1" x 1"

2" x 2"

1" x 1"

1" x 1"

2" x 3"

1" x 1"

2" x 2"

1" x 1"

2" x 2 3/4"

1" x 1"

1 3/4" x 1 3/4"

1" x 1"

2" x 2 3/4"

1" x 1"

1 3/4" x 1 3/4"

1" x 3"

1" x 1"

**For Each
Shamrock Block**

Shamrock Light
2—2" x 1 1/2"
2—2" x 2"

Shamrock Dark
2—2 3/4" x 2"
2—3" x 2"
1—3" x 1"

Background
13—1" x 1"
2—1 1/2" x 1 1/2"
2—1 1/2" x 2 3/4"
2—3/4" x 1 3/4"

Color Key
■ Dark green print
■ Light green print
□ Background

Shamrock Block
5" x 5" Block

1 1/2" x 1 1/2"

1 1/2" x 2 3/4"

Scrap Quilting Made Easy

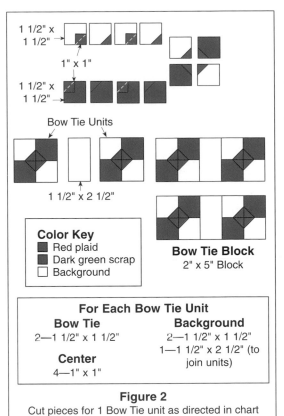

Bow Tie Units

1 1/2" x 2 1/2"

Color Key
- Red plaid
- Dark green scrap
- Background

Bow Tie Block
2" x 5" Block

For Each Bow Tie Unit

Bow Tie	Background
2—1 1/2" x 1 1/2"	2—1 1/2" x 1 1/2"
	1—1 1/2" x 2 1/2" (to join units)
Center	
4—1" x 1"	

Figure 2
Cut pieces for 1 Bow Tie unit as directed in chart referring to Color Key for fabrics. Piece units together as shown for 1 unit. Join 2 units with a 1 1/2" x 2 1/2" background piece for 1 block. Complete 4 blocks.

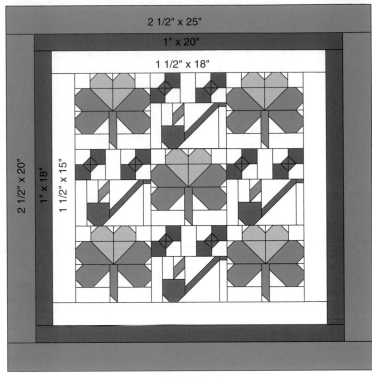

Bit o' Luck
Placement Diagram
25" x 25"

For Each Pipe Block

Smoke
1—1 1/4" x 2"

Pipe Block
1—3/4" x 1"
1—2" x 2"
1—2 3/4" x 3 1/2"

Background
1—1" x 1"
2—1 1/4" x 1 1/4"
1—1 1/4" x 2"
1—1 1/4" x 3 1/2"
1—2 1/2" x 2 1/2"
1—3 1/4" x 1"
1—3 1/4" x 3 1/4"

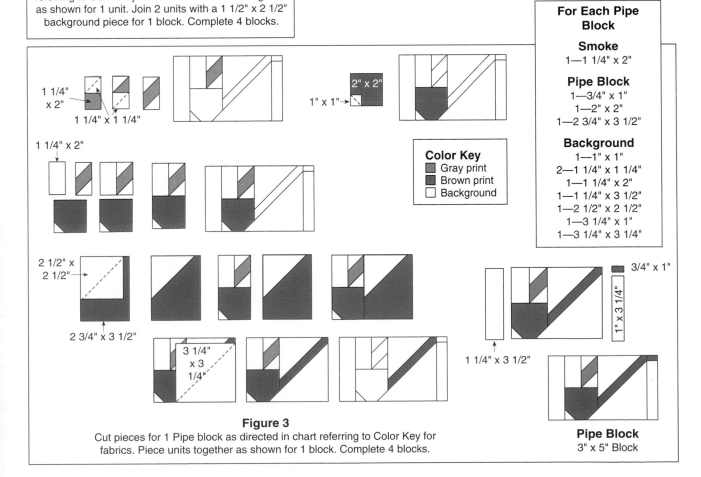

Color Key
- Gray print
- Brown print
- Background

Figure 3
Cut pieces for 1 Pipe block as directed in chart referring to Color Key for fabrics. Piece units together as shown for 1 block. Complete 4 blocks.

Pipe Block
3" x 5" Block

Easter Bouquet

Choose bright floral prints for the borders and matching scraps on the wreaths to make a wall quilt that will bring the color and beauty of spring flowers into your home.

QUILT SPECIFICATIONS
Skill Level: Intermediate
Quilt Size: 26 3/4" x 26 3/4"
Block Size: 7" x 7"
Number of Blocks: 4

MATERIALS
- Scrap bright green print for buds
- 1 fat quarter each rose and orange prints for small flowers
- 1 fat quarter purple print for large flowers
- 1 yard white-on-white print for background
- 1/4 yard green stripe for inside border
- 1/2 yard large floral print for outside border and binding
- All-purpose threads to match fabrics
- 1 spool clear nylon monofilament thread
- Backing 30" x 30"
- Batting 30" x 30"

Wreath Block
7" x 7"

Piecing the Blocks
Step 1. Cut pieces as directed in Figure 1 for small flower units referring to the Color Key, the photo and Placement Diagram for color suggestions.

Step 2. To piece a small flower unit, place a 1 1/2" x 1 1/2" rose or orange print square on a white-on-white background 1 1/2" x 2" rectangle. Sew across the diagonal as shown in Figure 1. Press back the stitched triangle; trim excess layers if desired; repeat for two units.

Step 3. Arrange the pieced units with cut units as shown in Figure 1; join to make one small flower unit; press. Repeat for two rose print and two orange print small flower units.

Step 4. Cut pieces as directed in Figure 2 for large flower units referring to the Color Key, the photo and Placement Diagram for color suggestions.

Step 5. To make tops of large flowers, sew a 1" x 1" white-on-white background square to a 1 1/2" x 1 1/2" green print square, referring to Figure 2; repeat for second square. Sew a 1" x 1 1/2" background rectangle to each side; press. Repeat for four of these units.

Step 6. Sew a 1 1/2" x 1 1/2" purple print square to each bottom corner of the previously pieced units; press. Trim away excess layers, if desired.

Step 7. Sew a 1 1/2" x 1 1/2" background square to each bottom corner of a purple print 2" x 2 1/2" piece; press. Repeat for four units.

Step 8. Sew one of these units to the bottom of the flower top units to complete a large flower unit; press. Repeat for four units.

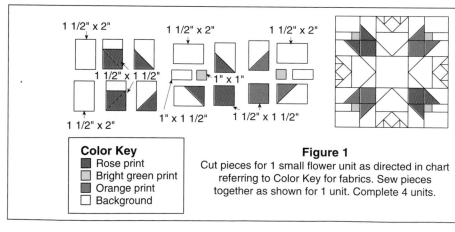

1 1/2" x 2"   1 1/2" x 2"   1 1/2" x 2"

1 1/2" x 1 1/2"   1" x 1"

1 1/2" x 2"   1" x 1 1/2"   1 1/2" x 1 1/2"

Color Key
- ▨ Rose print
- ▨ Bright green print
- ▨ Orange print
- ☐ Background

Figure 1
Cut pieces for 1 small flower unit as directed in chart referring to Color Key for fabrics. Sew pieces together as shown for 1 unit. Complete 4 units.

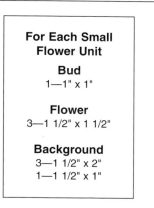

For Each Small Flower Unit

Bud
1—1" x 1"

Flower
3—1 1/2" x 1 1/2"

Background
3—1 1/2" x 2"
1—1 1/2" x 1"

Step 9. Cut a 2 1/2" x 2 1/2" white-on-white background square. Arrange the pieced units with this square in rows referring to Figure 2. Join the units in rows; join the rows to complete one block; press. Repeat for four blocks.

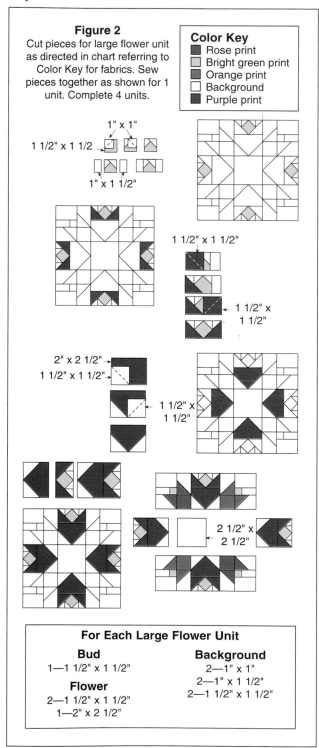

Figure 2
Cut pieces for large flower unit as directed in chart referring to Color Key for fabrics. Sew pieces together as shown for 1 unit. Complete 4 units.

Color Key
- Rose print
- Bright green print
- Orange print
- Background
- Purple print

1" x 1"

1 1/2" x 1 1/2

1" x 1 1/2"

1 1/2" x 1 1/2"

1 1/2" x 1 1/2"

2" x 2 1/2"
1 1/2" x 1 1/2"

1 1/2" x 1 1/2"

2 1/2" x 2 1/2"

For Each Large Flower Unit

Bud
1—1 1/2" x 1 1/2"

Flower
2—1 1/2" x 1 1/2"
1—2" x 2 1/2"

Background
2—1" x 1"
2—1" x 1 1/2"
2—1 1/2" x 1 1/2"

Assembly
Step 1. Cut one square each white-on-white background print 7 1/2" x 7 1/2" and 11 1/8" x 11 1/8" and two squares 5 7/8" x 5 7/8". Cut the 11 1/8" square in half on both diagonals to make side setting triangles as shown in Figure 3. Cut the 5 7/8" squares in half once on the diagonal to make corner triangles as shown in Figure 3.

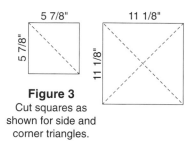

5 7/8"   11 1/8"

5 7/8"   11 1/8"

Figure 3
Cut squares as shown for side and corner triangles.

Step 2. Arrange the pieced blocks in diagonal rows with the 7 1/2" square and corner and setting triangles as shown in Figure 4. Join in diagonal rows; join rows to complete center; press.

Figure 4
Arrange pieced blocks in diagonal rows with center square and triangles as shown.

Step 3. Cut two strips green stripe 1 1/2" x 20 1/4" and two strips 1 1/2" x 22 1/4". Sew short strips to sides and long strips to top and bottom; press seams toward strips.

Step 4. Cut two strips large floral print 3" x 22 1/4" and two strips 3" x 27 1/4". Sew the short strips to the sides and long strips to the top and bottom; press seams toward strips.

Finishing
Step 1. Prepare quilt top for quilting referring to instructions in Chapter 5.

Step 2. Quilt in the ditch of seams and as desired

by machine using clear nylon monofilament thread in the top of the machine and thread to match backing in the bobbin.

Step 3. Prepare 3 1/4 yards binding from large floral print and finish edges referring to Chapter 5 for instructions.

—By Lisa Christensen

2 1/2" x 26 3/4"

1" x 21 3/4"

2 1/2" x 21 3/4"

1" x 19 3/4"

Welcome Wreath
Placement Diagram
26 3/4" x 26 3/4"

MAY DAY
Pocketful of Posies

Dig into the scrap bag for pieces to make this basket quilt to celebrate May Day. Use each fabric at least twice if you want a coordinated look. The small appliqué templates and yo-yo flowers will use some of your smallest scraps. We've included the template for a bow, but you could add a three-dimensional bow and hang this quilt on point.

QUILT SPECIFICATIONS
Skill Level: Intermediate
Quilt Size: 42" x 42"

MATERIALS
- Scraps green solid and prints, yellow solid and prints and blue and pink prints
- 1/4 yard multicolored print
- 3/4 yard pink plaid (borders, basket and flowers)
- 2 1/2 yards blue floral print (center, backing, outer border, flowers)
- 1 package 1/2"-wide pink single-fold bias tape
- Paper-backed fusible transfer web
- Thread: neutral all-purpose and rayon threads to coordinate with scraps
- 1 spool neutral quilting thread
- 1 spool nylon monofilament
- 2 1/2 yards green rat-tail cord
- Assorted buttons
- Navy pearl cotton
- Navy embroidery floss
- Seam sealant
- Black fine-point permanent marker
- Cotton quilt batting 46" x 46"
- Basic sewing supplies, tracing paper, rotary cutter, mat and ruler

PROJECT NOTES
All seam allowances are 1/4".

If pearl cotton is too thick to pass easily through dense fabrics, use 3 strands of embroidery floss instead.

INSTRUCTIONS
Step 1. Prewash all fabrics; press to remove excess wrinkles.

Step 2. Cut one 18 1/2" x 18 1/2" square blue floral print for center and two strips 6 1/2" x 30 1/2" and two strips 6 1/2" x 42 1/2" for outer borders. Cut four strips 6 1/2" x 18 1/2" pink plaid for inner

borders and four 6 1/2" x 6 1/2" squares yellow print for corner blocks.

Step 3. Place tracing paper over patterns; trace and cut out.

Step 4. Bond fusible web to wrong side of chosen fabric scraps, following manufacturer's instructions. Place patterns facedown on paper side of bonded fabrics. Trace as indicated on patterns; cut out. Remove paper backing.

Step 5. Place basket base on one corner of the center square 2" from each side as shown in Figure 1; pin in place. Position bias binding for handle with ends under edge of basket base with center 7 3/4" from basket center. Stitch handle in place with blind-hem or zigzag stitch using monofilament thread. Fuse basket base in place.

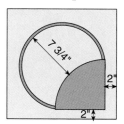

Figure 1
Place basket on center square.

Step 6. Position A, B and C pieces on the basket base using dotted lines on pattern as guides for placement; fuse in place. Position bow on handle; fuse in place. Satin-stitch around each piece with coordinating rayon thread.

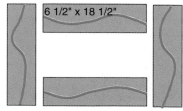

Figure 2
Place cording on inner border pieces.

Step 7. Place green cord on inner border pieces, as shown in Figure 2. Stitch in place with blind-hem

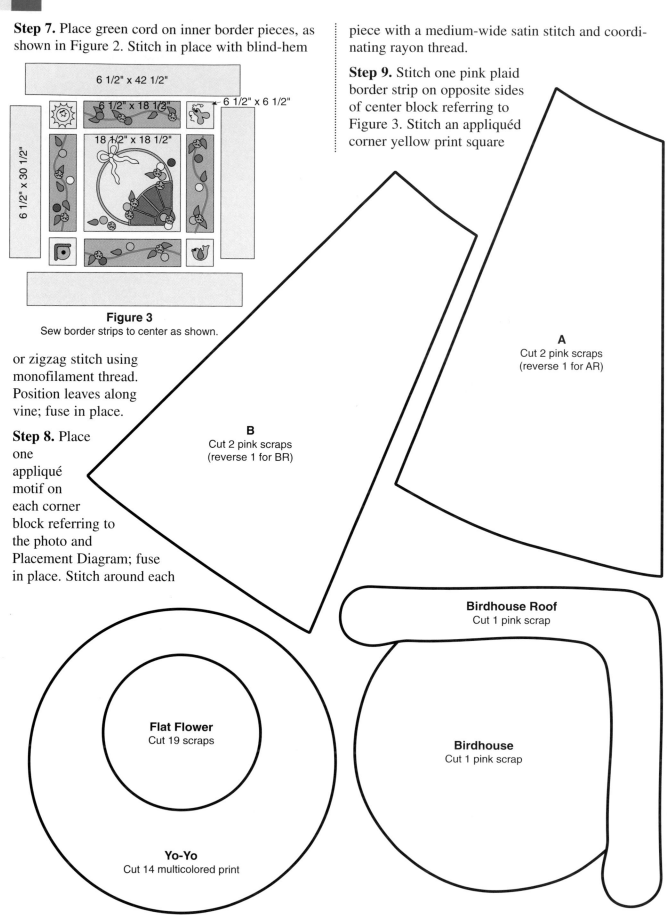

Figure 3
Sew border strips to center as shown.

or zigzag stitch using monofilament thread. Position leaves along vine; fuse in place.

Step 8. Place one appliqué motif on each corner block referring to the photo and Placement Diagram; fuse in place. Stitch around each

piece with a medium-wide satin stitch and coordinating rayon thread.

Step 9. Stitch one pink plaid border strip on opposite sides of center block referring to Figure 3. Stitch an appliquéd corner yellow print square

A
Cut 2 pink scraps
(reverse 1 for AR)

B
Cut 2 pink scraps
(reverse 1 for BR)

Birdhouse Roof
Cut 1 pink scrap

Flat Flower
Cut 19 scraps

Birdhouse
Cut 1 pink scrap

Yo-Yo
Cut 14 multicolored print

on each end of two remaining border strips referring to photo and Placement Diagram.

Step 10. Pin one strip along top edge and one along bottom edge, matching border seams as shown in Figure 3. Stitch; press seam allowances toward borders.

Step 11. Stitch 6 1/2" x 30 1/2" blue print outer border strip to opposite sides; stitch and press. Stitch the 6 1/2" x 42 1/2" blue print strips to top and bottom; press.

Step 12. Place yo-yo pattern on multicolored print fabric with no fusible web. Trace 14 yo-yos; cut out. Turn raw edge under 1/8" and work a running stitch along fold using quilting thread. Pull to gather into a puff referring to Figure 5; flatten puff with hand.

Step 13. Arrange flat flowers and yo-yos around basket and along vines referring to the Placement

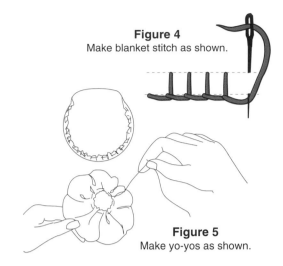

Figure 4
Make blanket stitch as shown.

Figure 5
Make yo-yos as shown.

Diagram and project photo. Pin, then fuse flat flowers in place. Pin, then stitch yo-yos in place through the centers. Work blanket stitch around flat flowers using pearl cotton referring to Figure 4.

Pocketful of Posies
Placement Diagram
42" x 42"

Finishing

Step 1. Cut backing and batting 1" larger all around than quilt top. Sandwich; pin; quilt around shapes and seams by machine using monofilament thread in the top of the machine and all-purpose thread to match backing in the bobbin.

Step 2. Trim batting even with quilt top. Trim backing to 3/4" larger all around for binding. Fold excess backing in half; wrap fold to front, mitering corners. Pin through all layers; stitch in place with zigzag stitch and monofilament thread.

Step 3. Stitch a two-hole button in the center of

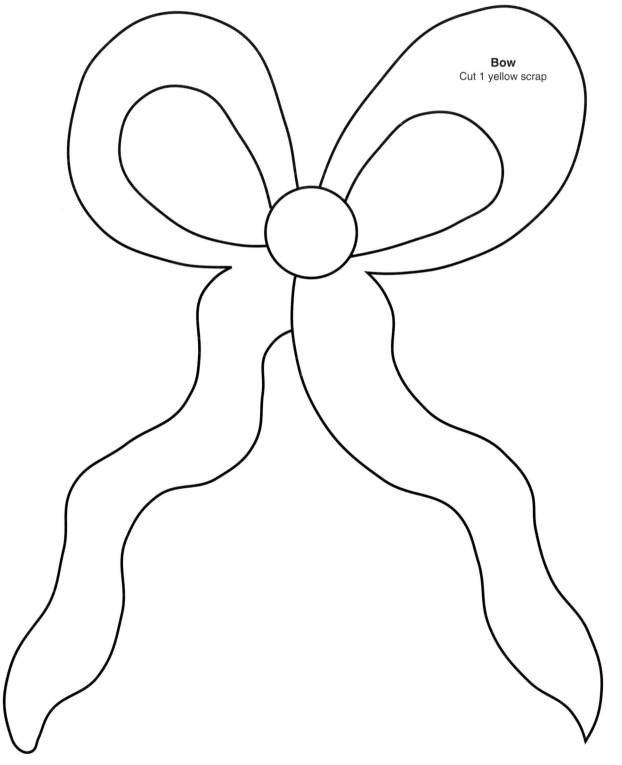

Bow
Cut 1 yellow scrap

each flower using embroidery floss. Knot ends; apply a drop of seam sealant to secure. Trim, leaving ends 1/2" long. Secure yo-yos with knots, eliminating the buttons.

Step 4. Add sun's face and butterfly antennae with permanent marker. Stitch one dark shank button for bird's eye, hole in birdhouse and butterfly's head referring to photo of project for placement.

—By Beth Wheeler

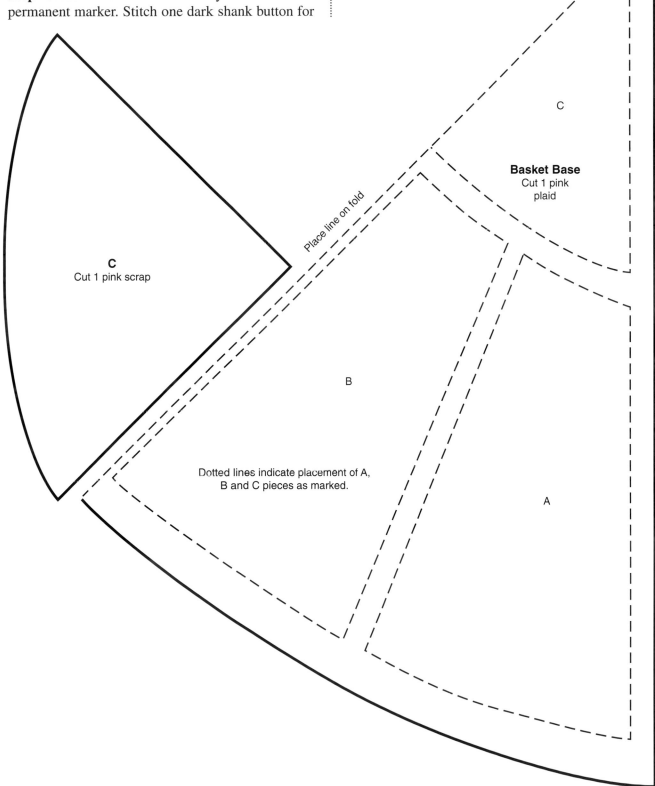

C

Basket Base
Cut 1 pink plaid

C
Cut 1 pink scrap

Place line on fold

B

Dotted lines indicate placement of A, B and C pieces as marked.

A

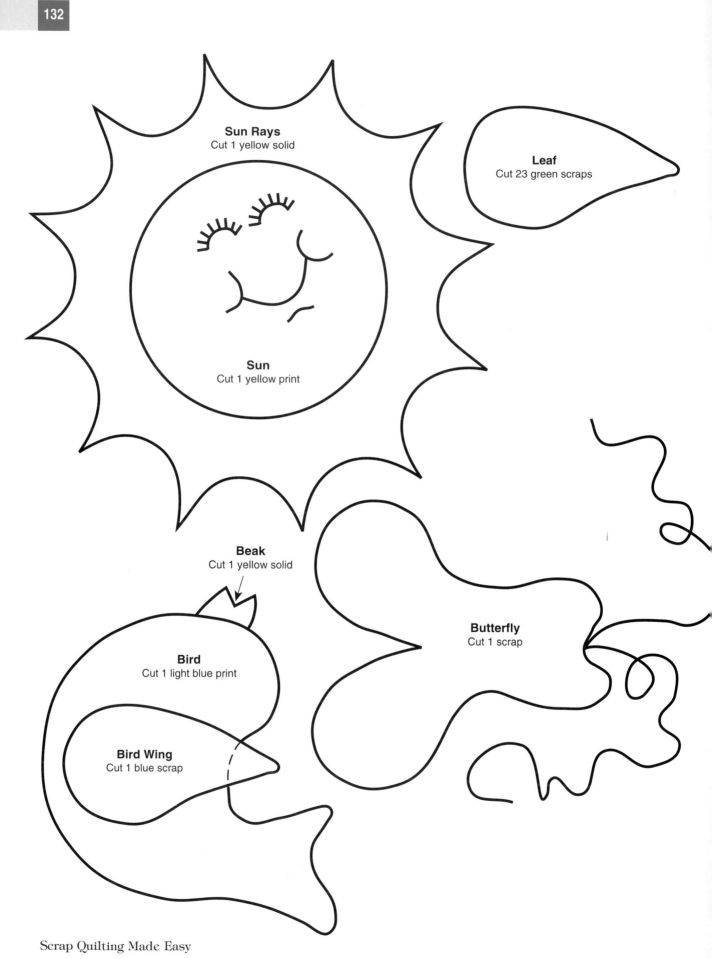

Sun Rays
Cut 1 yellow solid

Leaf
Cut 23 green scraps

Sun
Cut 1 yellow print

Beak
Cut 1 yellow solid

Butterfly
Cut 1 scrap

Bird
Cut 1 light blue print

Bird Wing
Cut 1 blue scrap

Quilting on a Star

Collect a galaxy of star prints to make this patriotic jacket and celebrate the Fourth of July with a bang. Use your favorite jacket pattern to create this striking garment.

PROJECT SPECIFICATIONS
Skill Level: Beginner

Jacket Size: Any size

MATERIALS
- Jacket pattern of choice
- Star prints to total 1 yard more than pattern requirements
- Lining fabric per pattern requirements
- All-purpose threads to match fabrics

INSTRUCTIONS
Step 1. Prepare a template using the pattern piece given. Cut diamond shapes from scrap fabrics using template. ***Note:** The back of the jacket shown has 64 diamonds, each front has 40 diamonds and each sleeve has approximately 70 diamonds (total approximately 348 diamonds).*

Step 2. Lay out paper pattern for the jacket front. Arrange diamonds on pattern in a pleasing design as shown in Figure 1. Cover entire pattern with enough left on all edges for seams, taking into account seams to join rows.

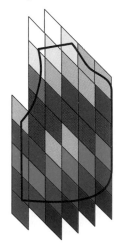

Figure 1
Cover paper pattern with diamonds,
arranging in a pleasing design.

Step 3. Pin the diamonds together in rows; mark each row with a number for sequence to join as

shown in Figure 2. Join the rows; press seams in one direction.

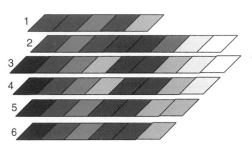

Figure 2
Sew diamonds together in
rows; number the rows. Sew
rows to create diamond fabric.

Step 4. Place paper pattern on pieced diamond fabric; cut using pattern cutting lines as shown in Figure 3.

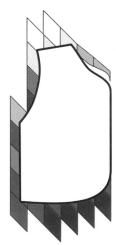

Figure 3
Place paper pattern on top of pieced
diamond fabric; cut on pattern lines.

Step 5. Repeat, turning pattern over for opposite front side. Try to match the sequence of the pieces and seams on both sides as shown in Figure 4.

Step 6. Lay out pattern back piece. Arrange diamonds on pattern starting at the center back, making both sides meet in the center and the colors repeat as shown in Figure 5. Create diamond fabric as in Step 3 and cut as in Step 4.

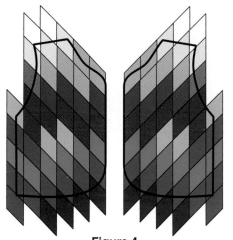

Figure 4
Reverse pattern for opposite side,
matching piecing sequence as shown.

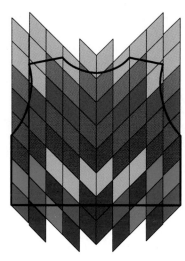

Step 7. Repeat arrangement, cutting and piecing procedures for each sleeve.

Step 8. Finish jacket using cut pieces as directed in the pattern instructions for jacket.

—By Ann Boyce

Figure 5
Lay out star patches with pieces meeting as
shown for center back of jacket. Pin and join
in rows. Join the rows to create pattern.

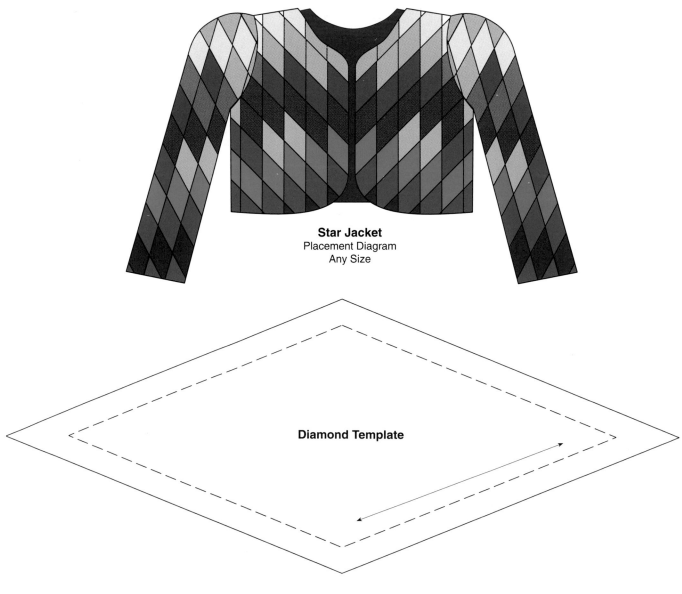

Star Jacket
Placement Diagram
Any Size

Diamond Template

Father's Day Vest

Even if you are a novice sewer, you can make this vest for your father or husband. Select plaids to make a masculine-looking vest that any style-conscious man could wear with or without a jacket.

PROJECT SPECIFICATIONS

Skill Level: Beginner

Vest Size: Any size

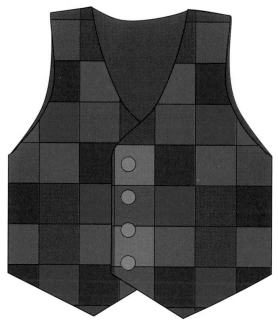

Father's Day Vest
Placement Diagram

MATERIALS

- 7/8 yard check for lining
- 3/4 yard plaid for vest back
- 10 (1/8-yard) pieces dark plaid
- Men's commercial vest pattern
- Neutral color all-purpose thread
- 4 (1") buttons
- Basic sewing supplies and tools

INSTRUCTIONS

Step 1. Prewash all fabrics; press.

Step 2. Cut 70 squares 4" x 4" from dark plaid fabrics.

Step 3. Sew 35 squares together as shown in Figure 1 for one vest front. Repeat in reverse for second vest front.

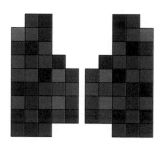

Figure 1
Sew squares together to make 2 sections as shown.

Step 4. Lay commercial vest front pattern on each pieced section as shown in Figure 2. Add more squares in any area needed if pieced section is not large enough. Cut vest front shapes from pieced sections.

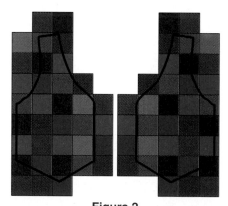

Figure 2
Lay vest front pattern on each section; cut out shape.

Step 5. Cut vest lining and back; finish the vest following instructions given with the commercial pattern.

—By Ann Boyce

School Daze Vest

Whether it's worn by a student who's learning reading, writing and arithmetic, or by a teacher who's teaching to the tune of a hickory stick, this vest gets an A+.

INSTRUCTIONS

Step 1. Using purchased pattern, cut right and left vest fronts from solid color fabric. Cut right and left vest fronts from plaid or print fabric for lining. Cut two back pieces, one for lining.

Step 2. Prepare templates using pattern pieces given.

Step 3. Fuse transfer web to wrong side of fabric scraps. Trace appliqué shapes onto paper side of fusible transfer web.

Step 4. Cut out appliqué pieces from fabric scraps.

Step 5. Place cutout schoolhouse pieces on the right vest front and apples on the left vest front referring to the Placement Diagram and photo of finished vest for suggested arrangement; layer pieces as necessary. Remove paper; fuse in place following manufacturer's instructions.

Step 6. Using 3 strands of black embroidery floss and a blanket stitch (Figure 1), stitch around outside edges of all appliqué shapes.

Figure 1
Make blanket stitch as shown using 3 strands of floss.

Step 7. Assemble vest according to purchased pattern instructions.

Step 8. Hand-sew the doorknob button and bell in place as marked on pattern pieces.

Step 9. Using embroidery floss, stitch a 1/4" running stitch around front outside edges and armholes through all thicknesses to finish.

—By LaRayne Meyer

PROJECT SPECIFICATIONS

Skill Level: Beginner

Vest Size: Any size

MATERIALS

- Purchased vest pattern without front darts
- Yardage needed for vest as listed on pattern; solid color front and plaid or print vest back and facing for vest front
- 3 different scraps of fabric in coordinating prints and plaids
- 1 skein black embroidery floss
- 1 spool all-purpose thread to match vest fabrics
- Paper-backed fusible transfer web
- Tiny gold ball button for doorknob
- Small gold bell

Support for Cupola
Cut 2

Cupola
Cut 1

Bell

School Daze Vest
Placement Diagram

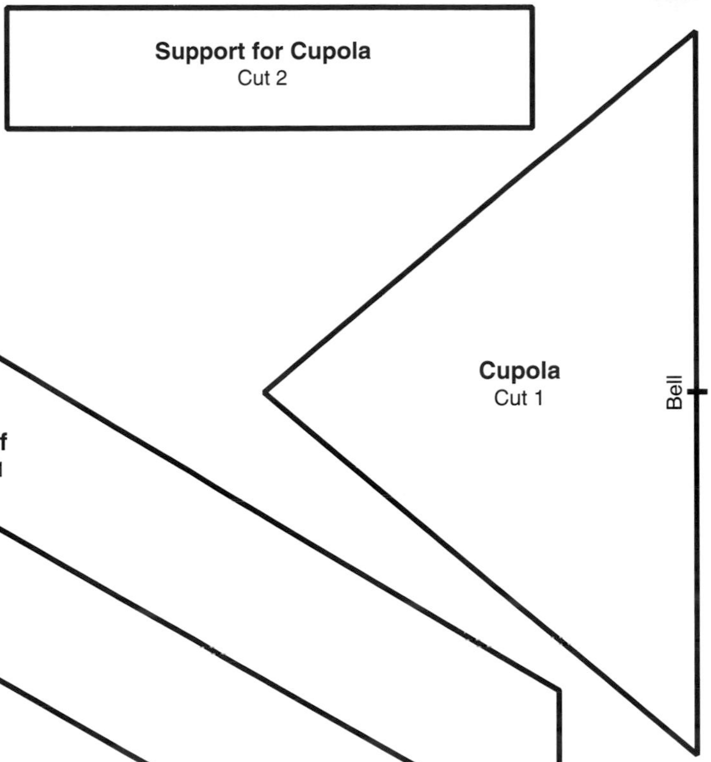

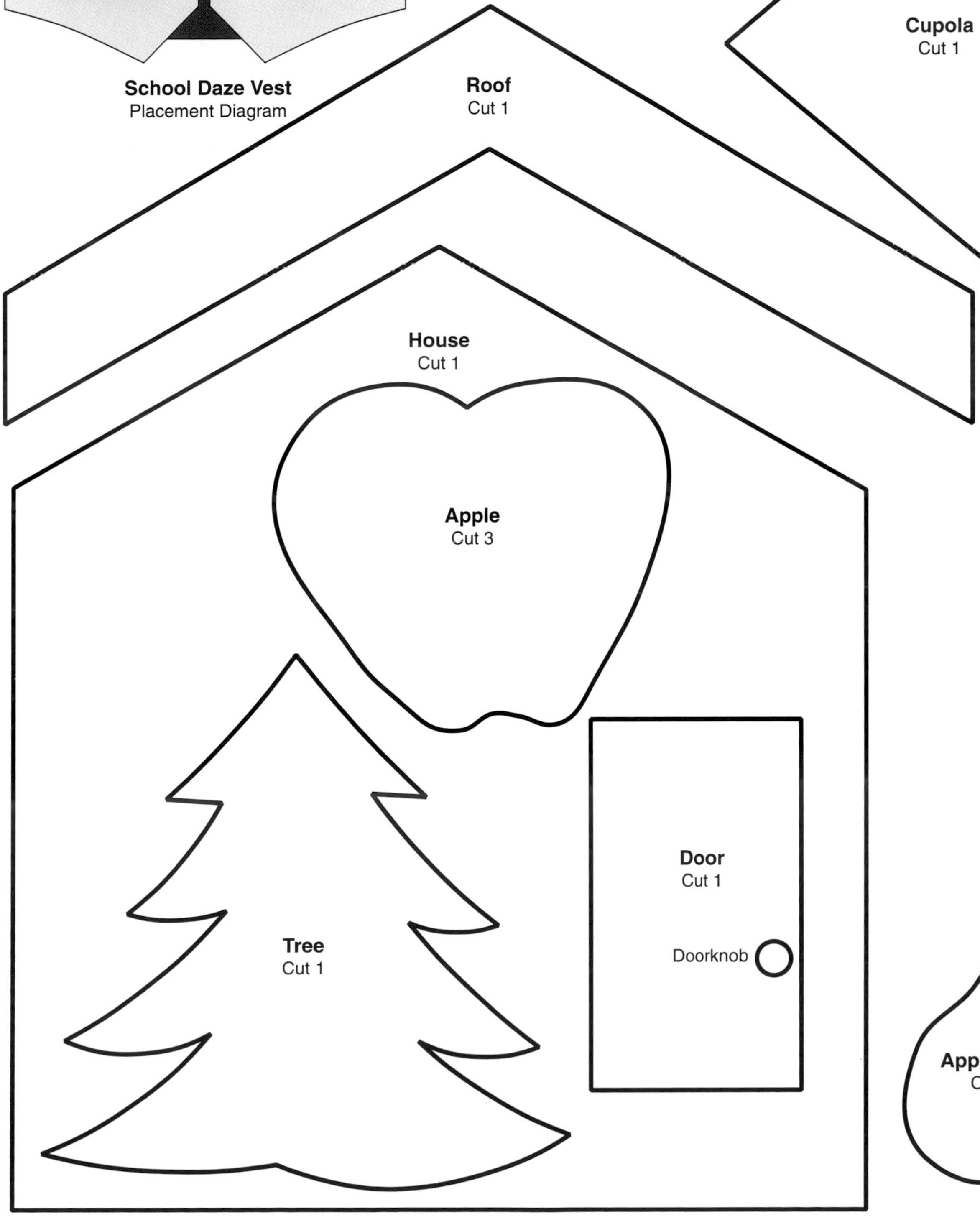

Roof
Cut 1

House
Cut 1

Apple
Cut 3

Door
Cut 1

Doorknob

Tree
Cut 1

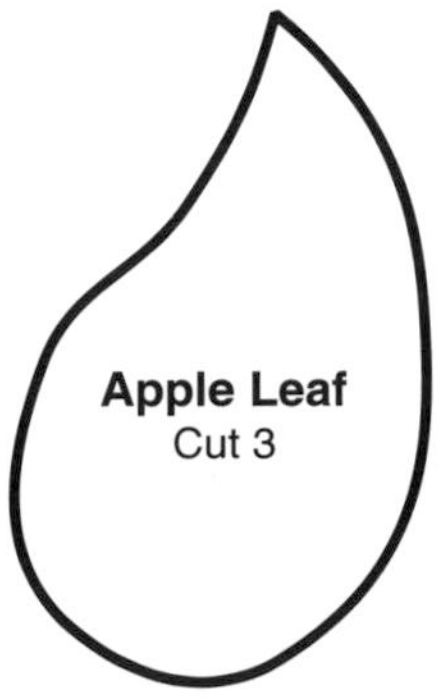

Apple Leaf
Cut 3

Little Red Schoolhouse Quilt

That special teacher will love having a schoolhouse
wall quilt to welcome children and visitors to her classroom.

PROJECT SPECIFICATIONS
Skill Level: Beginner

Quilt Size: Approximately 18" x 20"

MATERIALS
- 1 piece red plaid 18" x 20"
- Scraps red, blue, green, gold and white solids, red and tan plaids, red pin dot and red print
- Red-and-white stripe backing piece 22" x 24"
- Batting 22" x 24"
- Fusible transfer web
- Yellow embroidery floss
- 1 spool white all-purpose thread
- Coordinating rayon thread
- 1 spool nylon monofilament thread
- 3 small curtain rings
- Black fine-point permanent marker
- Basic sewing tools and supplies, tracing paper, white chalk pencil and embroidery needle

INSTRUCTIONS
Step 1. Cut a piece of tracing paper 18" x 20". Draw background shape referring to Figure 1. Cut and remove shaded triangles as shown in Figure 2 for a full-size pattern.

Step 2. Cut one background shape actual size from red plaid. Cut one 1" larger than pattern all around from red-and-white stripe backing piece; set side.

Step 3. Place tracing paper over patterns given; cut out.

Step 4. Bond fusible transfer web to wrong side of fabric scraps following manufactur-

er's instructions. Place patterns facedown on fabric scraps as directed on pattern pieces. Trace; cut out. Remove paper backing.

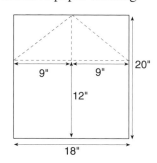

Figure 1
Draw lines on tracing paper
to make pattern for
background as shown.

Figure 2
Cut away shaded area
to complete pattern.

Step 5. Draw one triangle on tracing paper referring to Figure 3 for instructions. Use this pattern to cut one shape from tan plaid scrap.

Figure 3
Make a triangle using measurements given.

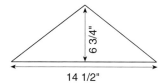

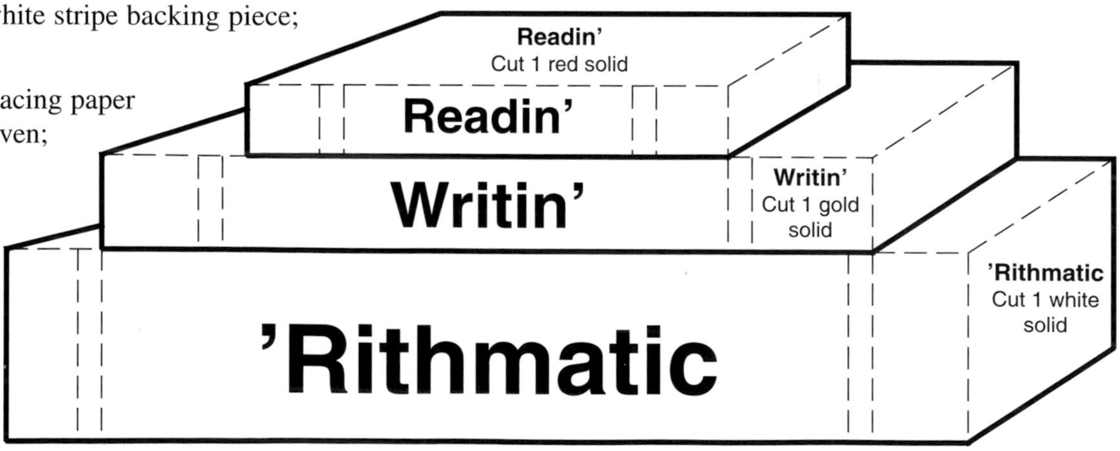

Readin'
Cut 1 red solid

Readin'

Writin'
Cut 1 gold
solid

Writin'

'Rithmatic
Cut 1 white
solid

'Rithmatic

Step 6. Cut one 6 1/2" x 7 1/4" rectangle from fused blue fabric and one from fused red pin dot. Cut one 4" x 14 1/2" piece green solid from fused fabric.

Step 7. Remove paper backing from fabrics. Arrange blocks on red plaid schoolhouse referring to the photograph, Placement Diagram and Figure 4 for arrangement; fuse in place. *Note: The red plaid background should be evenly visible on sides and bottom with about 1" left at top edges.*

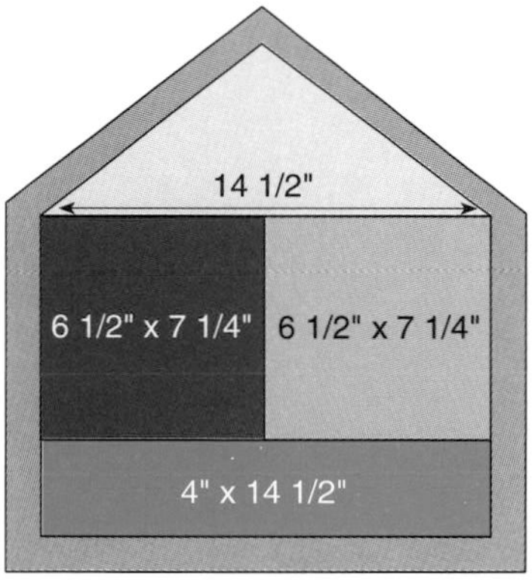

14 1/2"

6 1/2" x 7 1/4"   **6 1/2" x 7 1/4"**

4" x 14 1/2"

Figure 4
Arrange pieces as shown.

Step 8. Satin-stitch around each shape using red rayon thread in the top of the machine and white all-purpose thread in the bobbin.

Step 9. Fuse shapes on blocks referring to photo and Placement Diagram. Satin-stitch around each shape using matching rayon thread in the top of the machine and white thread in the bobbin. Using black fine-point permanent marker, transfer words and marks to book pieces.

Step 10. Mark message on green section using white chalk pencil and pattern.

Step 11. Sandwich batting between red plaid schoolhouse piece and red-and-white stripe backing piece; pin or baste to hold.

Step 12. Quilt around each shape and block using monofilament thread in the top of the machine and in the bobbin.

Step 13. Work message in running stitch with embroidery needle and 3 strands yellow floss.

Step 14. Trim batting only even with quilt top edge. Cut quilt backing 3/4" larger than red plaid schoolhouse all around. Fold backing edge over 1/4"; fold over top edge to encase batting and raw edges. Stitch in place using a narrow zigzag stitch and monofilament thread.

Step 15. Hand-stitch small rings on back of quilt for hanging to finish.

—By Beth Wheeler

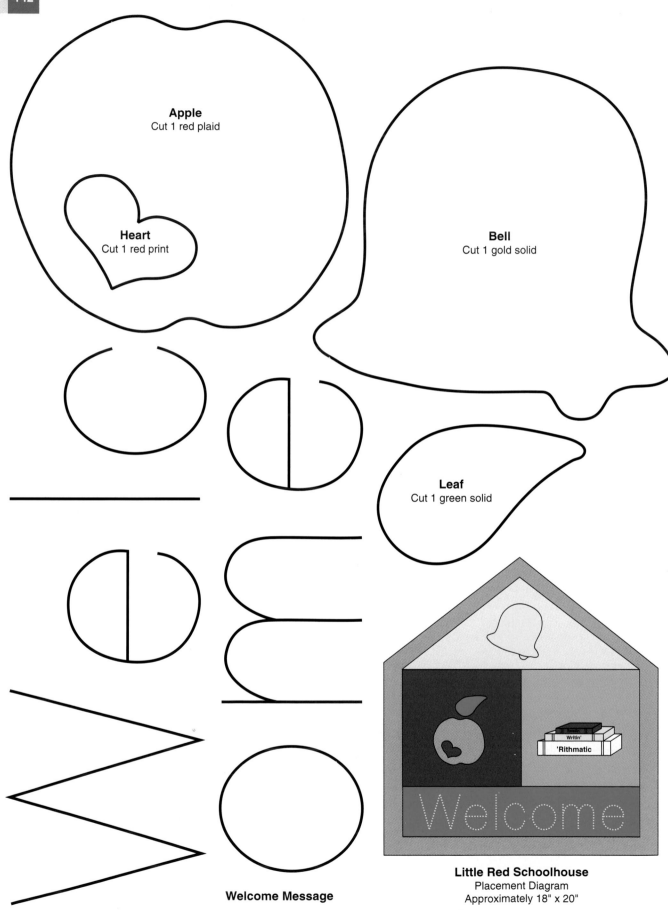

Apple
Cut 1 red plaid

Heart
Cut 1 red print

Bell
Cut 1 gold solid

Leaf
Cut 1 green solid

Welcome Message

Little Red Schoolhouse
Placement Diagram
Approximately 18" x 20"

Thanksgiving Hostess Set

Coordinate your scraps to make this hostess apron and a matching table runner.
The country blues and reds are a pleasing combination for every holiday of the year.

PROJECT SPECIFICATIONS
Skill Level: Intermediate
Table Runner Size: 16" x 58"
Apron: One size fits all

MATERIALS
Table Runner
- 16 pieces assorted print scraps each 4" x 9 1/2" for fan blades
- 2 red solid squares 4 1/2" x 4 1/2" for fan centers
- 8 pieces assorted prints 2 1/2" x 42 1/2" for center strips
- 2 squares fusible interfacing 4 1/2" x 4 1/2"
- Backing 18" x 60"
- Batting 18" x 60"
- 4 yards self-made or purchased binding

Apron
- 8 pieces assorted print scraps each 4" x 9 1/2" for fan blades
- 1 red solid square 4 1/2" x 4 1/2" for fan center
- 1 strip white print 2 1/2" x 16 1/2" for bottom of fan
- 2 squares red solid 8" x 8" for pocket
- 1 square each fusible interfacing 4 1/2" x 4 1/2" and 8" x 8"
- Backing 12" x 17"
- Batting 12" x 17"
- 1 1/8 yards blue print for skirt, waistband and ties
- 2" x 36" strip tear-off stabilizer
- 1 yard self-made or purchased binding

Both Projects
- 1 spool all-purpose thread to match backing
- 1 spool red thread to match red solid fabric
- 1 spool clear nylon monofilament thread

Table Runner

Step 1. Prepare fan templates using pattern pieces given. Cut as directed on fan blade piece for table runner.

Step 2. Join eight fan blade pieces as shown in Figure 1; press seams to one side as they are sewn. *Note: The bottom of the fan should measure 16 1/2" when sewn and pressed.* Repeat for second fan shape.

Figure 1
Piece fan blades
together as shown.

Step 3. Press fusible interfacing to wrong side of red solid squares; cut out fan center. Pin in place, centered at the bottom of the fan blades as shown in Figure 2.

Figure 2
Appliqué fan center over blades.

Step 4. Machine satin-stitch around outside edge of heart shapes using matching thread. From under-

Figure 3
Trim excess fabric from under fan center.

neath, cut away excess fabric under the fan centers to reduce bulk as shown in Figure 3.

Step 5. Sew the eight 2 1/2" x 42 1/2" fabric strips together along long edges in a pleasing arrangement; press seams to one side.

Step 6. Sew a pieced fan section to each end; press seams toward strips.

Step 7. Sandwich the batting piece between the completed table runner top and the prepared backing piece; pin or baste layers together to hold flat.

Step 8. Quilt as desired by machine using clear nylon threaded through the top of the machine and all-purpose thread to match backing in the bobbin.

Step 9. Bind outside edges using narrow self-made or purchased binding referring to Chapter 5 to finish.

Apron

Step 1. Prepare fan and apron pocket templates using pattern pieces given.

Step 2. Piece one fan section with fan center as for table runner. Sew the 2 1/2" x 16 1/2" strip across bottom as shown in Figure 4.

Figure 4
Sew the 2 1/2" x 16 1/2" strip to
the bottom of the fan shape.

Step 3. Sandwich the piece of batting between the stitched top and the prepared backing piece; pin or baste layers to hold flat.

Step 4. Quilt as desired by machine using clear nylon threaded through the top of the machine and all-purpose thread to match backing in the bobbin; set aside.

Step 5. Cut the following pieces from blue print: for skirt—22" x 36"; for waistband/ties—two strips 6" x 45"; for bib strap—4" x 22".

Step 6. To make skirt, press under a double 1/4" hem on both short sides as shown in Figure 5; topstitch. Sew a row of gathering stitches 1/4" and 1/2" from top edge; mark center referring to Figure 6.

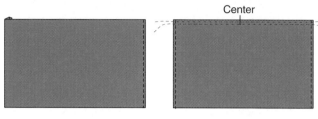

Figure 5
Fold under a double 1/4"
hem on skirt sides.

Figure 6
Sew 2 rows of gathering stitches
across top; mark center.

Step 7. Sew the two waistband/ties together on one short end; press seam open. Measure and mark 9" on each side of center seam as shown in Figure 7.

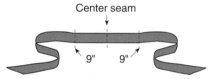

Figure 7
Mark 9" on each side of waistband/tie seam.

Step 8. With right sides together and raw edges even, match centers and sides of skirt to 9" marks referring to Figure 8. Pull gathers to fit; stitch top of skirt to waistband.

Apron
Placement Diagram

Table Runner
Placement Diagram
16" x 58"

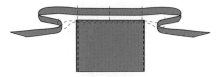

Figure 8
Match center and sides of
skirt to 9" marks.

Step 9. Fold each tie end in half lengthwise with right sides together; sew diagonally across ends and along length until you meet apron/waistband edge; turn right side out; press. Press under 1/4" on raw edge of remaining waistband section; slipstitch in place on wrong side of waistband, enclosing seam.

Step 10. Using pattern provided, cut out two pockets from red solid. Fuse interfacing to back of one section. Sew with right sides together, leaving an opening to turn along flat edge.

Step 11. Turn, press and slipstitch opening closed.

Step 12. Position on apron skirt 4" from left side and 4" down from waistband; topstitch between X's.

Step 13. To make bib strap, fold strap piece in half along long edge with right sides together. Stitch long side and across one end; turn and press.

Step 14. Turn in raw edge on other end of strip; slipstitch. Sew both ends to apron bib at edges of center fan blades, referring to the Placement Diagram.

Step 15. Center completed bib 1/4" under edge of waistband; topstitch in place.

Step 16. Use the top edges of the fan center as a pattern to trace scallops on bottom edge of apron skirt. Straight-stitch over these marks. Trim fabric

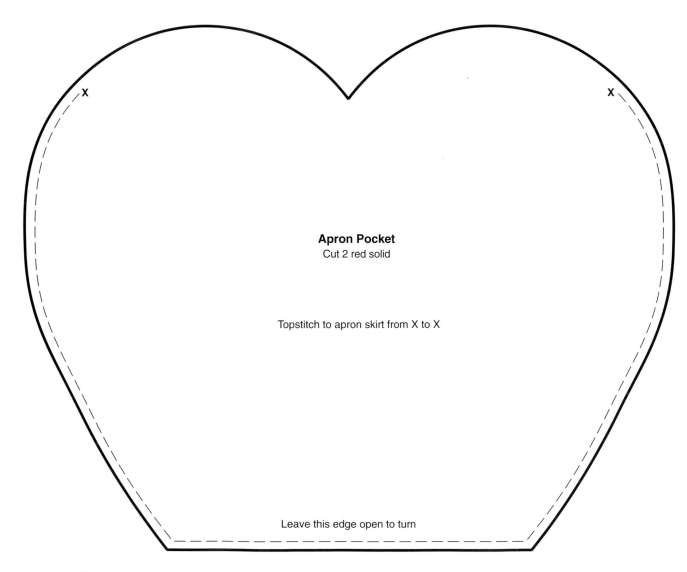

X   X

Apron Pocket
Cut 2 red solid

Topstitch to apron skirt from X to X

Leave this edge open to turn

to edge of stitching; machine satin-stitch over the stitching with tear-off stabilizer underneath as shown in Figure 9. Trim threads; remove stabilizer to finish.

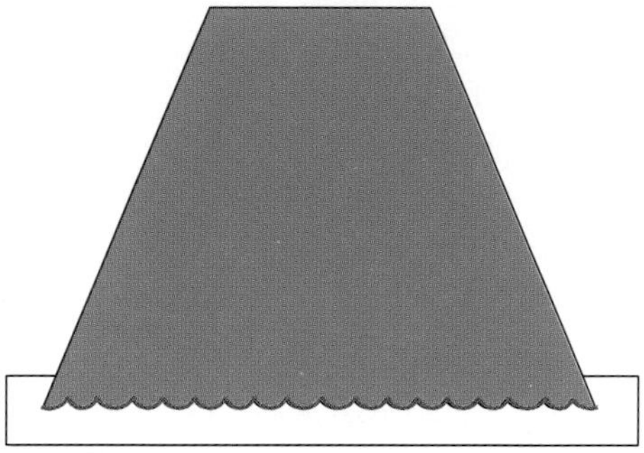

Figure 9
Place stabilizer under skirt bottom;
stitch along marked lines to make
a scalloped edge.

—By Karen Neary

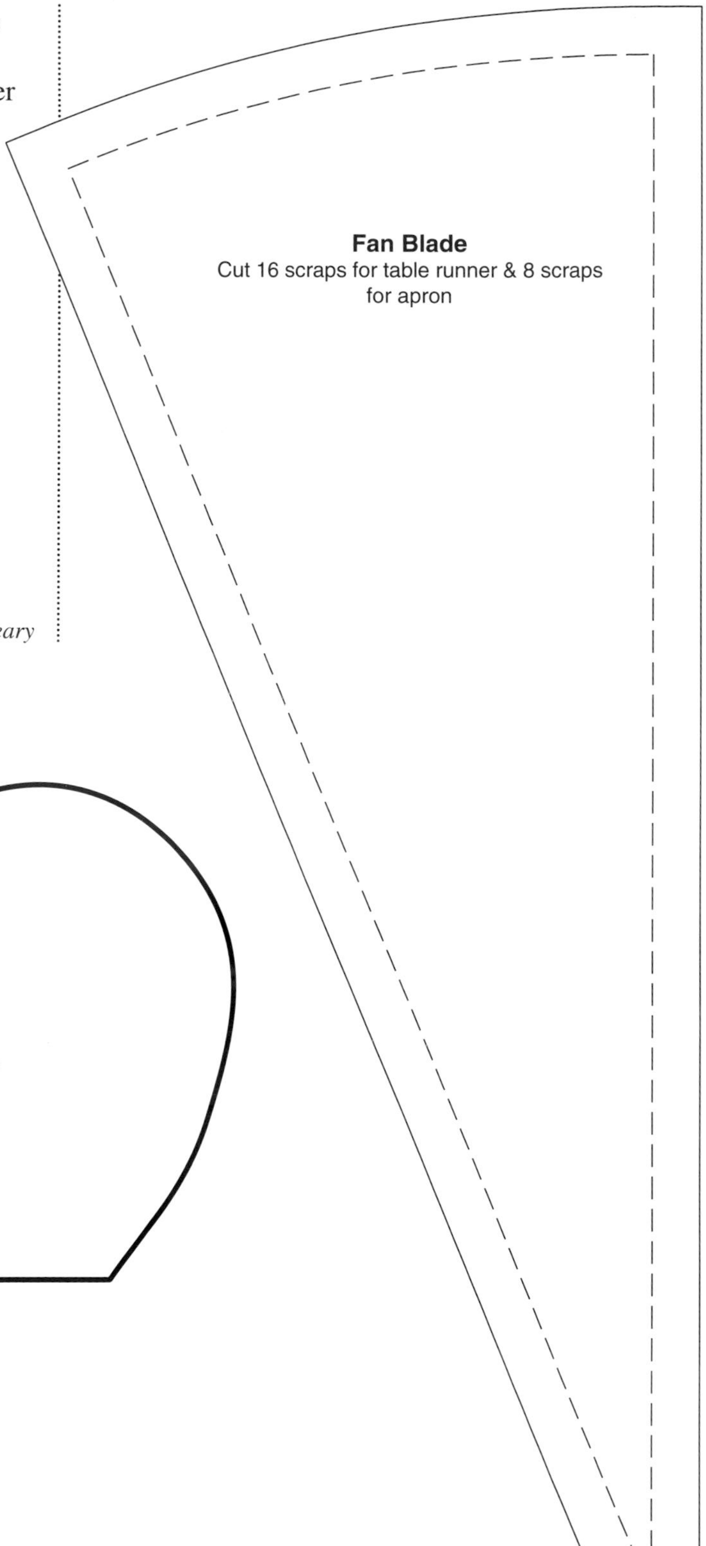

Fan Blade
Cut 16 scraps for table runner & 8 scraps
for apron

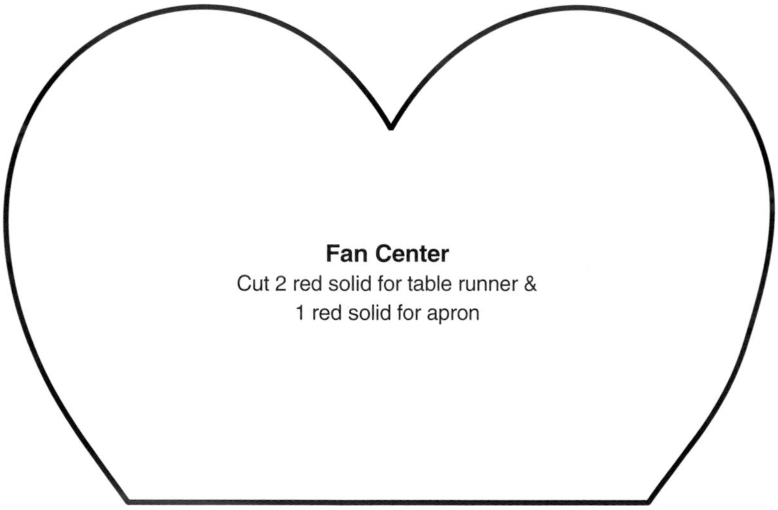

Fan Center
Cut 2 red solid for table runner &
1 red solid for apron

General Instructions

Quiltmaking Basics
Materials & Supplies

FABRICS

Fabric Choices. Scrap quilts combine fabrics of many types, depending on the quilt. Antique crazy quilts combined silk, wool and cotton. This combination requires special care and use because some fabrics are more fragile than others. It is best to combine same-fiber-content fabrics when making scrap quilts.

Buying Fabrics. One hundred percent cotton fabrics are recommended for making quilts. Choose colors similar to those used in the quilts shown or colors of your own preference. Most scrap quilt designs depend more on contrast of values than on the colors used to create the design.

Preparing the Fabric for Use. Fabrics may be prewashed depending on your preference. Whether you prewash or not, be sure your fabrics are color-fast and won't run onto each other when washed after use.

Fabric Grain. Fabrics are woven with threads going in a crosswise and lengthwise direction. The threads cross at right angles—the more threads per inch, the stronger the fabric.

The crosswise threads will stretch a little. The lengthwise threads will not stretch at all. Cutting the fabric at a 45-degree angle to the crosswise and lengthwise threads produces a bias edge which stretches a great deal when pulled (Figure 1).

If templates are given with patterns in this book, pay careful attention to the grain lines marked with arrows. These arrows indicate that the piece should be placed on the lengthwise grain with the arrow running on one thread. Although it is not necessary to examine the fabric and find a thread to match to, it is important to try to place the arrow with the lengthwise grain of the fabric (Figure 2).

THREAD

For most piecing, good-quality cotton or cotton-covered polyester is the thread of choice. Inexpensive polyester threads are not recommended because they can cut the fibers of cotton fabrics.

Choose a color thread that will match or blend with the fabrics in your quilt. Most scrap quilts are pieced with dark and light color fabrics. Choose a neutral thread color, such as a medium gray, as a compromise between colors. Test by pulling a sample seam.

BATTING

Batting is the material used to give a quilt loft or thickness. It also adds warmth.

Batting size is listed in inches for each pattern to reflect the size needed to complete the quilt according to the instructions. Purchase the size large enough to cut the size you need for the quilt of your choice.

Some qualities to look for in batting are drapability, resistance to fiber migration, loft and softness.

If you are unsure which kind of batting to use, purchase the smallest size batting available in the type you'd like to try. Test each sample on a small project. Choose the batting that you like working with most and that will result in the type of quilt you need.

TOOLS & EQUIPMENT

There are few truly essential tools and little equipment required for quiltmaking. Basics include needles (hand-sewing and quilting betweens), pins (long, thin sharp pins are best), sharp scissors or shears, a thimble, template materials (plastic or cardboard), marking tools (chalk marker, water-erasable pen and a No. 2 pencil are a few) and a quilting frame or hoop. For piecing and/or quilting by machine, add a sewing machine to the list.

Other sewing basics such as a seam ripper, pincushion, measuring tape and an iron are also necessary. For choosing colors or quilting designs for

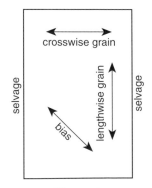

Figure 1
Drawing shows lengthwise, crosswise and bias threads.

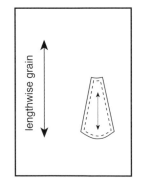

Figure 2
Place the template with marked arrow on the lengthwise grain of the fabric.

your quilt, or for designing your own quilt, it is helpful to have on hand graph paper, tracing paper, colored pencils or markers and a ruler.

For making scrap quilts, a rotary cutter, mat and specialty rulers are often used. We recommend an ergonomic rotary cutter, a large self-healing mat and several rulers. If you can choose only one size, a 6" x 24" marked in 1/8" or 1/4" increments is recommended.

Construction Methods

Traditional Templates. While some quilt instructions in this book use rotary-cut strips and quick sewing methods, many patterns require a template. Templates are like the pattern pieces used to sew a garment. They are used to cut the fabric pieces which make up the quilt top. There are two types— templates that include a 1/4" seam allowance and those that don't.

Choose the template material and the pattern. Transfer the pattern shapes to the template material with a sharp No. 2 lead pencil. Write the pattern name, piece letter or number, grain line and number to cut for one block or whole quilt on each piece as shown in Figure 3.

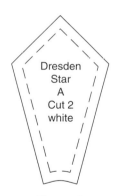

Figure 3
Mark each template with the pattern name and piece identification.

Some patterns require a reversed piece (Figure 4). These patterns are labeled with an R after the piece letter; for example, B and BR. To reverse a template, first cut it with the labeled side up and then with the labeled side down. Compare these to the right and left fronts of a blouse. When making a garment, you accomplish reversed pieces when cutting the pattern on two layers of fabric placed with right sides together. This can be done when cutting templates as well.

If cutting one layer of fabric at a time, first trace the template onto the backside of the fabric with the marked side down; turn the template over with the marked side up to make reverse pieces.

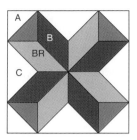

Figure 4
This pattern uses reversed pieces.

Hand-Piecing Basics. When hand-piecing it is easier to begin with templates which do not include the 1/4" seam allowance. Place the template on the wrong side of the fabric, lining up the marked grain line with lengthwise or crosswise fabric grain. If the piece does not have to be reversed, place with labeled side up. Trace around shape; move, leaving 1/2" between the shapes, and mark again.

When you have marked the appropriate number of pieces, cut out pieces, leaving 1/4" beyond marked line all around each piece.

Patterns in this book include a drawing suggesting the assembly order. Refer to these drawings to piece units and blocks.

To join two units, place the patches with right sides together. Stick a pin in at the beginning of the seam through both fabric patches, matching the beginning points (Figure 5); for hand-piecing, the seam begins on the traced line, not at the edge of the fabric (see Figure 6).

Figure 5
Stick a pin through fabrics to match the beginning of the seam.

Figure 6
Begin hand-piecing at seam, not at the edge of the fabric. Continue stitching along seam line.

Thread a sharp needle; knot one strand of the thread at the end. Remove the pin and insert the needle in the hole; make a short stitch and then a backstitch right over the first stitch. Continue making short stitches with several stitches on the needle at one time. As you stitch, check the back piece often to assure accurate stitching on the seam line. Take a stitch at the end of the seam; backstitch and knot at the same time as shown in Figure 7. Seams on hand-pieced fabric patches may be finger-pressed toward the darker fabric.

To sew units together, pin fabric patches together, matching seams. Sew as above except where seams meet; at these intersections, backstitch, go through seam to next piece and backstitch again to secure seam joint.

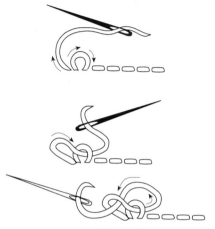

Figure 7
Make a loop in a backstitch to make a knot.

Not all pieced blocks can be stitched with straight seams or in rows. Some patterns require set-in pieces. To begin a set-in seam, pin one side of the square to the proper side of the star point with right sides together, matching corners. Start stitching at the seam line on the outside point; stitch on the marked seam line to the end of the seam line at the center referring to Figure 8.

Bring around the adjacent side and pin to the next star point, matching seams. Continue the stitching line from the adjacent seam through corners and to the outside edge of the square as shown in Figure 9.

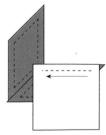

Figure 8
To set a square into a diamond point, match seams and stitch from outside edge to center.

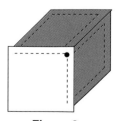

Figure 9
Continue stitching the adjacent side of the square to the next diamond shape in 1 seam from center to outside as shown.

Machine-Piecing. If making templates, include the 1/4" seam allowance on the template for machine-piecing. Place template on the wrong side of the fabric as for hand-piecing except butt pieces against one another when tracing.

Set machine on 2.5 or 12–15 stitches per inch. Join pieces as for hand-piecing for set-in seams; but for other straight seams, begin and end sewing at the end of the fabric patch sewn as shown in Figure 10. No backstitching is necessary when machine-stitching.

Join units as for hand-piecing referring to the piecing diagrams where needed. Chain piecing (Figure 11—sewing several like units before sewing other units) saves time by eliminating beginning and ending stitches.

When joining machine-pieced units, match seams against each other with seam allowances pressed in opposite directions to reduce bulk and make perfect matching of seams possible (Figure 12).

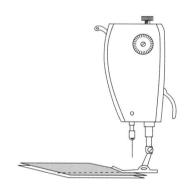

Figure 10
Begin machine-piecing at the end of the piece, not at the end of the seam.

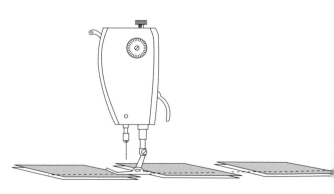

Figure 11
Units may be chain-pieced to save time.

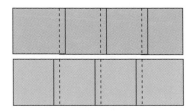

Figure 12
Sew machine-pieced units with seams
pressed in opposite directions.

Quick-Cutting. Quick-cutting and piecing strips is recommended for making many of the scrap quilts in this book. Templates are completely eliminated; instead, a rotary cutter, plastic ruler and mat are used to cut fabric strips.

When rotary-cutting strips, straighten raw edges of fabric by folding fabric in fourths across the width as shown in Figure 13. Press down flat; place ruler on fabric square with edge of fabric and make one cut from the folded edge to the outside edge. If strips are not straightened, a wavy strip will result as shown in Figure 14.

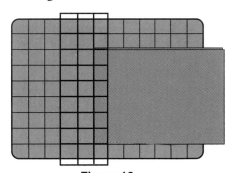

Figure 13
Fold fabric and straighten as shown.

Figure 14
Wavy strips result if fabric is not straightened before cutting.

Always cut away from your body, holding the ruler firmly with the non-cutting hand. Keep fingers away from the edge of the ruler as it is easy for the rotary cutter to slip and jump over the edge of the ruler if cutting is not properly done.

If a square is required for the pattern, it can be sub-cut from a strip as shown in Figure 15.

Figure 15
If cutting squares, cut proper-width strip into same-width segments. Here, a 2" strip is cut into 2" segments to create 2" squares. These squares finish at 1 1/2" when sewn.

If you need right triangles with the straight grain on the short sides, you can use the same method, but you need to figure out how wide to cut the strip. Measure the finished size of one short side of the triangle. Add 7/8" to this size for seam allowance. Cut fabric strips this width; cut the strips into the same increment to create squares. Cut the squares on the diagonal to produce triangles. For example, if you need a triangle with a 2" finished height, cut the strips 2 7/8" by the width of the fabric. Cut the strips into 2 7/8" squares. Cut each square on the diagonal to produce the correct-size triangle with the grain on the short sides (Figure 16).

Triangles sewn together to make squares are called half-square triangles or triangle/squares. When joined, the triangle/square unit has the straight of grain on all outside edges of the block.

Another method of making triangle/squares is shown in Figure 17. Layer two squares with right sides together; draw a diagonal line through the center. Stitch 1/4" on both sides of the line. Cut apart on the drawn line to reveal two stitched triangle/squares.

If you need triangles with the straight of grain on the diagonal, such as for fill-in triangles on the outside edges of a diagonal-set quilt, the procedure is a bit different.

To make these triangles, a square is cut on both diagonals; thus, the straight of grain is on the longest or diagonal side (Figure 18). To figure out the size to cut the square, add 1 1/4" to the needed finished size of the longest side of the triangle. For example, if you need a triangle with a 12" finished diagonal, cut a 13 1/4" square.

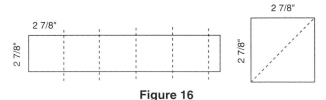

Figure 16
Cut 2" (finished size) triangles from 2 7/8" squares as shown.

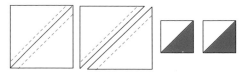

Figure 17
Mark a diagonal line on the square; stitch 1/4" on each side of the line. Cut on line to reveal stitched triangle/squares.

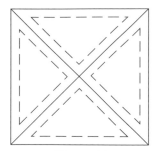

Figure 18
Add 1 1/4" to the finished size of the
longest side of the triangle needed
and cut on both diagonals to make a
quarter-square triangle.

If templates are given, use their measurments to cut fabric strips to correspond with that measurement. The template may be used on the strip to cut pieces quickly. Strip cutting works best for squares, triangles, rectangles and diamonds. Odd-shaped templates are difficult to cut in multiple layers or using a rotary cutter.

Quick-Piecing Method. Lay pieces to be joined under the presser foot of the sewing machine right sides together. Sew an exact 1/4" seam allowance to the end of the piece; place another unit right next to the first one and continue sewing, adding a piece after every stitched piece, until all of the pieces are used up (Figure 19).

When sewing is finished, cut threads joining the pieces apart. Press seam toward the darker fabric.

Figure 19
Sew pieces together in a chain.

Foundation Piecing. Paper or fabric foundation pieces are used to make very accurate blocks, provide stability for weak fabrics, and add body and weight to the finished quilt.

Temporary foundation materials include paper, tracing paper, freezer paper and removable interfacing. Permanent foundations include utility fabrics, non-woven interfacing, flannel, fleece and batting.

Methods of marking foundations include basting lines, pencils or pens, needlepunching, tracing wheel, hot-iron transfers, copy machine, pre-marked, stamps or stencils.

There are two methods of foundation piecing— under-piecing and top-piecing. When under-piecing, the pattern is reversed when tracing. We have not included any patterns for top-piecing.

Note: All patterns for which we recommend paper piecing are already reversed in full-size drawings given.

To under-piece, place a scrap of fabric larger than the lined space on the unlined side of the paper in the No. 1 position. Place piece 2 right sides together with piece 1; pin on seam line, and fold back to check that the piece will cover space 2 before stitching.

Stitch along line on the lined side of the paper— fabric will not be visible. Sew several stitches beyond the beginning and ending of the line. Backstitching is not required as another fabric seam will cover this seam.

Remove pin; finger-press piece 2 flat. Continue adding all pieces in numerical order in the same manner until all pieces are stitched to paper. Trim excess to outside line (1/4" larger all around than finished size of the block).

Tips & Techniques

If you cannot see the lines on the back-side of the paper when paper-piecing, draw over lines with a small felt-tip marker. The lines should now be visible on the backside to help with placement of fabric pieces.

Before machine-piecing fabric patches together, test your sewing machine for positioning an accurate 1/4" seam allowance. There are several tools to help guarantee this. Some machine needles may be moved to allow the presser-foot edge to be a 1/4" guide.

A special foot may be purchased for your machine that will guarantee an accurate 1/4" seam. A piece of masking tape can be placed on the throat plate of your sewing machine to mark the 1/4" seam. A plastic stick-on ruler may be used instead of tape with the same results.

Tracing paper can be used as a temporary foundation. It is removed when blocks are complete and stitched together. To paper-piece, copy patterns given here using a copy machine or trace each block individually. Measure the finished paper foundations to insure accuracy in copying.

Putting It All Together

Many steps are required to prepare a quilt top for quilting, including setting the blocks together, adding borders, choosing and marking quilting designs, layering the top, batting and backing for quilting, quilting or tying the layers and finishing the edges of the quilt.

As you begin the process of finishing your quilt top, strive for a neat, flat quilt with square sides and corners, not for perfection—that will come with time and practice.

Finishing the Top

Settings. Most quilts are made by sewing individual blocks together in rows which, when joined, create a design. There are several other methods used to join blocks. Sometimes the setting choice is determined by the block's design. For example, a house block should be placed upright on a quilt, not sideways or upside down.

Plain blocks can be alternated with pieced or appliquéd blocks in a straight set. Making a quilt using plain blocks saves time; half the number of pieced or appliquéd blocks are needed to make the same-size quilt as shown in Figure 1.

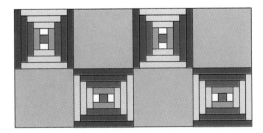

Figure 1
Alternate plain blocks with pieced blocks to save time.

Adding Borders. Borders are an integral part of the quilt and should complement the colors and designs used in the quilt center. Borders frame a quilt just like a mat and frame do a picture.

If fabric strips are added for borders, they may be mitered or butted at the corners as shown in Figures 2 and 3. To determine the size for butted border strips, measure across the center of the completed quilt top from one side raw edge to the other side raw edge. This measurement will include a 1/4" seam allowance.

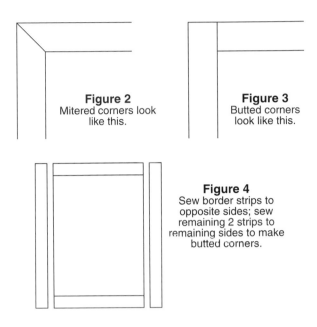

Figure 2
Mitered corners look like this.

Figure 3
Butted corners look like this.

Figure 4
Sew border strips to opposite sides; sew remaining 2 strips to remaining sides to make butted corners.

Cut two border strips that length by the chosen width of the border. Sew these strips to the top and bottom of the pieced center referring to Figure 4. Press the seam allowance toward the border strips.

Measure across the completed quilt top at the center, from top raw edge to bottom raw edge, including the two border strips already added. Cut two border strips that length by the chosen width of the border. Sew a strip to each of the two remaining sides as shown in Figure 4. Press the seams toward the border strips.

To make mitered corners, measure the quilt as before. To this add twice the width of the border and 1/2" for seam allowances to determine the length of the strips. Repeat for opposite sides. Sew on each strip, stopping stitching 1/4" from corner, leaving the remainder of the strip dangling.

Press corners at a 45-degree angle to form a crease. Stitch from the inside quilt corner to the outside on the creased line. Trim excess away after stitching and press mitered seams open (Figures 5–7).

Carefully press the entire piece, including the

pieced center. Avoid pulling and stretching while pressing, which would distort shapes.

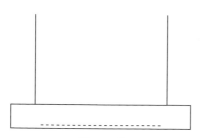

Figure 5
For mitered corner, stitch strip, stopping 1/4" from corner seam.

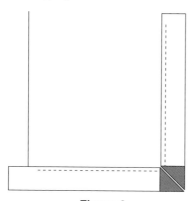

Figure 6
Fold and press corner to make a 45-degree angle.

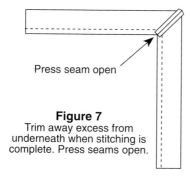

Press seam open

Figure 7
Trim away excess from underneath when stitching is complete. Press seams open.

Getting Ready to Quilt

Choosing a Quilting Design. If you choose to hand- or machine-quilt your finished top, you will need to choose a design for quilting.

There are several types of quilting designs, some of which may not have to be marked. The easiest of the unmarked designs is in-the-ditch quilting. Here the quilting stitches are placed in the valley created by the seams joining two pieces together or next to the edge of an appliqué design. There is no need to mark a top for in-the-ditch quilting. Machine quil-

ters choose this option because the stitches are not as obvious on the finished quilt. (Figure 8).

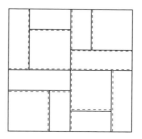

Figure 8
In-the-ditch quilting is done in the seam that joins 2 pieces.

Outline-quilting 1/4" or more away from seams or appliqué shapes is another no-mark alternative (Figure 9) which prevents having to sew through the layers made by seams, thus making stitching easier.

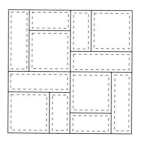

Figure 9
Outline-quilting 1/4" away from seam is a popular choice for quilting.

If you are not comfortable eyeballing the 1/4" (or other distance), masking tape is available in different widths and is helpful to place on straight-edge designs to mark the quilting line. If using masking tape, place the tape right up against the seam and quilt close to the other edge.

Meander or free-motion quilting by machine fills in open spaces and doesn't require marking. It is fun and easy to stitch as shown in Figure 10.

Figure 10
Machine meander quilting fills in large spaces.

Marking the Top for Quilting or Tying. If you choose a fancy or allover design for quilting, you will need to transfer the design to your quilt top before layering with the backing and batting. You may use a sharp medium-lead or silver pencil on light background fabrics. Test the pencil marks to guarantee that they will wash out of your quilt top when quilting is complete; or be sure your quilting stitches cover the pencil marks. Mechanical pencils with very fine points may be used successfully to mark quilts.

Manufactured quilt-design templates are available in many designs and sizes and are cut out of a durable plastic template material which is easy to use.

To make a permanent quilt-design template, choose a template material on which to transfer the design. See-through plastic is the best as it will let you place the design while allowing you to see where it is in relation to your quilt design without moving it. Place the design on the quilt top where you want it and trace around it with your marking tool. Pick up the quilting template and place again; repeat marking.

No matter what marking method you use, remember—the marked lines should *never show* on the finished quilt. When the top is marked, it is ready for layering.

Preparing the Quilt Backing. The quilt backing is a very important feature of your quilt. In most cases, the Materials list for each quilt in this book gives the size requirements for the backing, not the yardage needed. Exceptions to this are when the backing fabric is also used on the quilt top and yardage is given for that fabric.

A backing is generally cut at least 4" larger than the quilt top or 2" larger on all sides. For a 64" x 78" finished quilt, the backing would need to be at least 68" x 82".

To avoid having the seam across the center of the

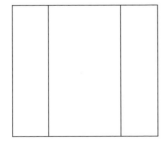

Figure 11
Center 1 backing piece with a piece on each side.

quilt backing, cut or tear one of the right-length pieces in half and sew half to each side of the second piece as shown in Figure 11.

Quilts that need a backing more than 88" wide may be pieced in horizontal pieces as shown in Figure 12.

Figure 12
Horizontal seams may be used on backing pieces.

Layering the Quilt Sandwich. Layering the quilt top with the batting and backing is time-consuming. Open the batting several days before you need it and place over a bed or flat on the floor to help flatten the creases caused from its being folded up in the bag for so long.

Iron the backing piece, folding in half both vertically and horizontally and pressing to mark centers.

If you will not be quilting on a frame, place the backing right side down on a clean floor or table. Start in the center and push any wrinkles or bunches flat. Use masking tape to tape the edges to the floor or large clips to hold the backing to the edges of the table. The backing should be taut.

Place the batting on top of the backing, matching centers using fold lines as guides; flatten out any wrinkles. Trim the batting to the same size as the backing.

Fold the quilt top in half lengthwise and place on top of the batting, wrong side against the batting, matching centers. Unfold quilt and, working from the center to the outside edges, smooth out any wrinkles or lumps.

To hold the quilt layers together for quilting, baste by hand or use safety pins. If basting by hand, thread a long thin needle with a long piece of unknotted white or off-white thread. Starting in the center and leaving a long tail, make 4"–6" stitches toward the outside edge of the quilt top, smoothing as you baste. Start at the center again and work toward the outside as shown in Figure 13.

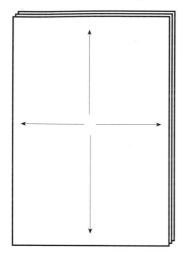

Figure 13
Baste from the center to the outside edges.

If quilting by machine, you may prefer to use safety pins for holding your fabric sandwich together. Start in the center of the quilt and pin to the outside, leaving pins open until all are placed.

When you are satisfied that all layers are smooth, close the pins.

Quilting

Hand Quilting. Hand quilting is the process of placing stitches through the quilt top, batting and backing to hold them together. While it is a functional process, it also adds beauty and loft to the finished quilt.

To begin, thread a sharp between needle with an 18" piece of quilting thread. Tie a small knot in the end of the thread. Position the needle about 1/2" to 1" away from the starting point on quilt top. Sink the needle through the top into the batting layer but not through the backing. Pull the needle up at the starting point of the quilting design. Pull the needle and thread until the knot sinks through the top into the batting (Figure 14).

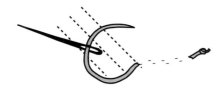

Figure 14
Start the needle through the top layer of fabric 1/2"–1" away from quilting line with knot on top of fabric.

Some stitchers like to take a backstitch here at the beginning while others prefer to begin the first stitch here. Take small, even running stitches along the marked quilting line (Figure 15). Keep one hand positioned underneath to feel the needle go all the way through to the backing.

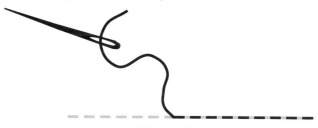

Figure 15
Make small, even running stitches on marked quilting line.

Machine Quilting. Successful machine quilting requires practice and a good relationship with your sewing machine.

Prepare the quilt for machine quilting in the same way as for hand-quilting. Use safety pins to hold the layers together instead of basting with thread.

Presser-foot quilting is best used for straight-line quilting because the presser bar lever does not need to be continually lifted.

Set the machine on a longer stitch length (three or eight to 10 stitches to the inch). Too tight a stitch

Protect Your Fingers

Use a thimble to prevent sore fingers when hand quilting. The finger that is under the quilt to feel the needle as it passes through the backing is the one that is most apt to get sore from the pin pricks. Some quilters purchase leather thimbles for this finger while others try home remedies. One simple aid is masking tape wrapped around the finger. With the tape you will still be able to feel the needle, but it will not prick your skin.

Over time calluses build up and these fingers get toughened up, but with every vacation from quilting, they will become soft and the process begins again.

When you feel your shoulder muscles tensing up, take a rest.

causes puckering and fabric tucks, either on the quilt top or backing. An even-feed or walking foot helps to eliminate the tucks and puckering by feeding the upper and lower layers through the machine evenly. Before you begin, loosen the amount of pressure on the presser foot.

Special machine-quilting needles work best to penetrate the three layers in your quilt. Decide on a design. Quilting in the ditch is not quite as visible, but if you quilt with the feed dogs engaged, it means turning the quilt frequently. It is not easy to fit a rolled-up quilt through the small opening on the sewing machine head.

Meander quilting is the easiest way to machine-quilt—and it is fun. Meander quilting is done using an appliqué or darning foot with the feed dogs dropped. It is sort of like scribbling. Simply move the quilt top around under the foot and make stitches in a random pattern to fill the space. The same method may be used to outline a quilt design. The trick is the same as in hand-quilting; you are striving for stitches of uniform size. Your hands are in complete control of the design.

If machine-quilting is of interest to you, there are several very good books available at quilt shops that will help you become a successful machine quilter.

Tied Quilts, or Comforters. Would you rather tie your quilt layers together than quilt them? Tied quilts are often referred to as comforters. The advantage of tying is that it takes so much less time and the required skills can be learned quickly.

If a top will be tied, choose a thick, bonded batting—one that will not separate during washing. For tying, use pearl cotton, embroidery floss, or strong yarn in colors that match or coordinate with the fabrics in your quilt top.

Decide on a pattern for tying. Many quilts are tied at the corners and centers of the blocks and at sashing joints. Try to tie every 4"–6". Special designs can be used for tying, but most quilts are tied in conventional ways. Begin tying in the center and work to the outside edges.

To make the tie, thread a large needle with a long thread (yarn, floss or crochet cotton); do not knot. Push the needle through the quilt top to the back, leaving a 3"–4" length on top. Move the needle to the next position without cutting thread. Take another stitch through the layers; repeat until thread is almost used up.

Cut thread between stitches, leaving an equal amount of thread on each stitch. Tie a knot with the two thread ends. Tie again to make a square knot referring to Figure 16. Trim thread ends to desired length.

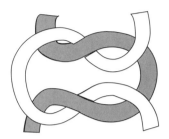

Figure 16
Make a square knot as shown.

Hand Quilting Hints

Knots should not show on the quilt top or back. Learn to sink the knot into the batting at the beginning and ending of the quilting thread for successful stitches. Making 12–18 stitches per inch is a nice goal, but a more realistic goal is seven to nine stitches per inch. If you cannot accomplish this right away, strive for even stitches—all the same size—that look as good on the back as on the front.

When you have nearly run out of thread, wind the thread around the needle several times to make a small knot and pull it close to the fabric. Insert the needle into the fabric on the quilting line and come out with the needle 1/2" to 1" away, pulling the knot into the fabric layers the same as when you started. Pull and cut thread close to fabric. The end should disappear inside after cutting. Some quilters prefer to take a backstitch with a loop through it for a knot to end.

You will perfect your quilting stitches as you gain experience, your stitches will get better with each project and your style will be uniquely your own.

Finishing the Edges

After your quilt is tied or quilted, the edges need to be finished. Decide how you want the edges of your quilt finished before layering the backing and batting with the quilt top.

Without Binding—Self-Finish. There is one way to eliminate adding an edge finish. This is done before quilting. Place the batting on a flat surface. Place the pieced top right side up on the batting. Place the backing right sides together with the pieced top. Pin and/or baste the layers together to hold flat referring to page 155.

Begin stitching in the center of one side using a 1/4" seam allowance, reversing at the beginning and end of the seam. Continue stitching all around and back to the beginning side. Leave a 12" or larger opening. Clip corners to reduce excess. Turn right side out through the opening. Slipstitch the opening closed by hand. The quilt may now be quilted by hand or machine.

The disadvantage to this method is that once the edges are sewn in, any creases or wrinkles that might form during the quilting process cannot be flattened out. Tying is the preferred method for finishing a quilt constructed using this method. Bringing the backing fabric to the front is another way to finish the quilt's edge without binding. To accomplish this, complete the quilt as for hand or machine quilting. Trim the batting *only* even with the front. Trim the backing 1" larger than the completed top all around.

Turn the backing edge in 1/2" and then turn over to the front along edge of batting. The folded edge may be machine-stitched close to the edge through all layers, or blind-stitched in place to finish.

The front may be turned to the back. If using this method, a wider front border is needed. The backing and batting are trimmed 1" *smaller* than the top and the top edge is turned under 1/2" and then turned to the back and stitched in place.

One more method of self-finish may be used. The top and backing may be stitched together by hand at the edge. To accomplish this, all quilting must be stopped 1/2" from the quilt-top edge. The top and backing of the quilt are trimmed even and the batting is trimmed to 1/4"–1/2" smaller. The edges of the top and backing are turned in 1/4"–1/2" and blind-stitched together at the very edge.

These methods do not require the use of extra fabric and save time in preparation of binding strips; they are not as durable as an added binding.

Binding. The technique of adding extra fabric at the edges of the quilt is called binding. The binding encloses the edges and adds an extra layer of fabric for durability.

To prepare the quilt for the addition of the binding, trim the batting and backing layers flush with the top of the quilt using a rotary cutter and ruler or shears. Using a walking-foot attachment (sometimes called an even-feed foot attachment), machine-baste the three layers together all around approximately 1/8" from the cut edge.

The list of materials given with each quilt in this book often includes a number of yards of self-made or purchased binding. Bias binding may be purchased in packages and in many colors. The advantage to self-made binding is that you can use fabrics from your quilt to coordinate colors. Double-fold, straight-grain binding and double-fold, bias-grain binding are two of the most commonly used types of binding.

Double-fold, straight-grain binding is used on smaller projects with right-angle corners. Double-fold, bias-grain binding is best suited for bed-size quilts or quilts with rounded corners.

To make double-fold, straight-grain binding, cut 2"-wide strips of fabric across the width or down the length of the fabric totaling the perimeter of the quilt plus 10". The strips are joined as shown in Figure 17 and pressed in half wrong sides together along the length using an iron on a cotton setting with *no* steam.

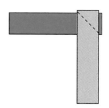

Figure 17
Join binding strips in a
diagonal seam to eliminate
bulk as shown.

Lining up the raw edges, place the binding on the top of the quilt and begin sewing (again using the walking foot) approximately 6" from the beginning of the binding strip. Stop sewing 1/4" from the first corner, leave the needle in the quilt, turn and sew diagonally to the corner as shown in Figure 18.

Fold the binding at a 45-degree angle up and away from the quilt as shown in Figure 19 and back down flush with the raw edges. Starting at the top raw edge of the quilt, begin sewing the next side as shown in Figure 20. Repeat at the next three corners.

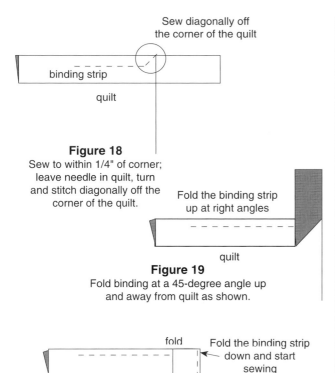

Figure 18
Sew to within 1/4" of corner;
leave needle in quilt, turn
and stitch diagonally off the
corner of the quilt.

Figure 19
Fold binding at a 45-degree angle up
and away from quilt as shown.

Figure 20
Fold the binding strips back
down, flush with the raw
edge, and begin sewing.

As you approach the beginning of the binding strip, stop stitching and overlap the binding 1/2" from the edge; trim. Join the two ends with a 1/4" seam allowance and press the seam open. Reposition the joined binding along the edge of the quilt and resume stitching to the beginning.

To finish, bring the folded edge of the binding over the raw edges and blind-stitch the binding in place over the machine-stitching line on the backside. Hand-miter the corners on the back as shown in Figure 21.

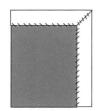

Figure 21
Miter and stitch the
corners as shown.

If you are making a quilt to be used on a bed, you will want to use double-fold, bias-grain bindings because the many threads that cross each other

along the fold at the edge of the quilt make it a more durable binding.

Cut 2"-wide bias strips from a large square of fabric. Join the strips as illustrated in Figure 17 and press the seams open. Fold the beginning end of the bias strip 1/4" from the raw edge and press. Fold the joined strips in half along the long side, wrong sides together, and press with *no* steam (Figure 22).

Figure 22
Fold end in and press strip in half.

Follow the same procedures as previously described for preparing the quilt top and sewing the binding to the quilt top. Treat the corners just as you treated them with straight-grain binding. Since you are using bias-grain binding, you do have the option to just eliminate the corners if this option doesn't interfere with the patchwork in the quilt. Round the corners off by placing one of your dinner plates at the corner and rotary-cutting the gentle curve (Figure 23).

Figure 23
Round corners to eliminate
square-corner finishes.

As you approach the beginning of the binding strip, stop stitching and lay the end across the beginning so it will slip inside the fold. Cut the end at a 45-degree angle so the raw edges are contained inside the beginning of the strip (Figure 24). Resume stitching to the beginning. Bring the fold to the back of the quilt and hand-stitch as previously described.

Figure 24
End the binding strips as shown.

Overlapped corners are not quite as easy as rounded ones, but a bit easier than mitering. To make overlapped corners, sew binding strips to opposite sides of the quilt top. Stitch edges down to finish. Trim ends even.

Sew a strip to each remaining side, leaving 1 1/2"–2" excess at each end. Turn quilt over and fold binding down even with previous finished edge as shown in Figure 25.

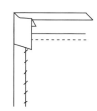

Figure 25
Fold end of binding even with previous edge.

Fold binding in toward quilt and stitch down as before, enclosing the previous bound edge in the seam. It may be necessary to trim the folded-down section to reduce bulk as shown in Figure 26.

Figure 26
An overlapped corner is not quite as neat as a mitered corner.

Final Touches

If your quilt will be hung on the wall, a hanging sleeve is required. Other options include purchased plastic rings or fabric tabs. The best choice is a fabric sleeve, which will evenly distribute the weight of the quilt across the top edge, rather than at selected spots where tabs or rings are stitched,

keep the quilt hanging straight and not damage the batting.

To make a sleeve, measure across the top of the finished quilt. Cut an 8"-wide piece of muslin equal to that length—you may need to seam several muslin strips together to make the required length.

Fold in 1/4" on each end of the muslin strip and press. Fold again and stitch to hold. Fold the muslin strip lengthwise with right sides together. Sew along the long side to make a tube. Turn the tube right side out; press with seam at bottom or centered on the back.

Hand-stitch the tube along the top of the quilt and the bottom of the tube to the quilt back making sure the quilt lies flat. Stitches should not go through to the front of the quilt and don't need to be too close together as shown in Figure 27.

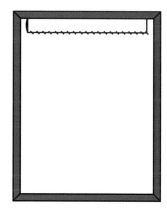

Figure 27
Sew a sleeve to the top back of the quilt.

Slip a wooden dowel or long curtain rod through the sleeve to hang.

When the quilt is finally complete, it should be signed and dated. Use a permanent pen on the back of the quilt. Other methods include cross-stitching your name and date on the front or back or making a permanent label which may be stitched to the back.